A Faith That Sings

Christ as priest forgives.
Christ as prophet guides.
Christ as king restores.

P 37 True religion is heart religion —
   God's grace for us and in us —
What kind of God does your doctrine
of salvation reveal?

$\mathcal{W}$esleyan Doctrine Series

The Wesleyan Doctrine Series seeks to reintroduce Christians in the Wesleyan tradition to the beauty of doctrine. The volumes in the series draw on the key sources for Wesleyan teaching: Scripture, Liturgy, Hymnody, the General Rules, the Articles of Religion and various Confessions. In this sense, it seeks to be distinctively Wesleyan. But it does this with a profound interest and respect for the unity and catholicity of Christ's body, the church, which is also distinctly Wesleyan. For this reason, the series supplements the Wesleyan tradition with the gifts of the church catholic, ancient, and contemporary. The Wesleyan tradition cannot survive without a genuine "Catholic Spirit." These volumes are intended for laity who have a holy desire to understand the faith they received at their baptism.

EDITORS:
Randy Cooper
Andrew Kinsey
D. Brent Laytham
D. Stephen Long

A Faith That Sings

Biblical Themes in the Lyrical Theology of Charles Wesley

PAUL W. CHILCOTE

With Questions for Consideration by Andrew Kinsey

CASCADE *Books* · Eugene, Oregon

A FAITH THAT SINGS
Biblical Themes in the Lyrical Theology of Charles Wesley

Wesleyan Doctrine Series 12

Cascade Books
An Imprint of Wipf and Stock Publishers
199 W. 8th Ave., Suite 3
Eugene, OR 97401

www.wipfandstock.com

PAPERBACK ISBN: 978-1-4982-3182-4
HARDCOVER ISBN: 978-1-4982-3184-8
EBOOK ISBN: 978-1-4982-3183-1

Cataloguing-in-Publication data:

Names: Chilcote, Paul Wesley, 1954–. | Kindsey, Andrew.

Title: A faith that sings : biblical themes in the lyrical theology of Charles Wesley / Paul W. Chilcote ; with questions for consideration by Andrew Kinsey.

Description: Eugene, OR : Cascade Books, 2016 | Series: Wesleyan Doctrine 12 | Includes bibliographical references.

Identifiers: ISBN 978-1-4982-3182-4 (paperback) | ISBN 978-1-4982-3184-8 (hardcover) | ISBN 978-1-4982-3183-1 (ebook)

Subjects: LCSH: Wesley, Charles, 1707–1788. | Methodist Church—Doctrines. | Hymns, English—History and criticism.

Classification: BX8495.W4 C465 2016 (print) | BX8495.W4 C465 (ebook)

Manufactured in the U.S.A.   NOVEMBER 14, 2016

For my friends and colleagues
in The Charles Wesley Society,
who have helped me cultivate
"a heart to praise my God"

Contents

Acknowledgments

THE SEED FOR THIS book was planted in my mind when I assisted in the preparation of *A Collection of Hymns for the People Called Methodists*, volume 7 in The Works of John Wesley. I was a graduate student at the time working on my dissertation under the direction of Dr. Frank Baker at Duke University. The power and beauty of Charles Wesley's hymns captured my soul. I have tried to emulate Professor Baker over the years by studying and publishing about both John and Charles Wesley, not just one or the other. But I confess that I have done all I can to get Charles out from under the shadow of his older brother, who tends to get most of the press and all of the credit. When I first learned about this series on Wesleyan doctrine and the vision of my colleagues concerning it, I just wanted to make sure that Charles Wesley found a rightful place in it. So I am very grateful to the editors for the opportunity to make this contribution.

I served for eight years as president of The Charles Wesley Society. This Society was formed in 1990, primarily through the efforts of S T Kimbrough Jr., for the "study, preservation, interpretation, and dissemination of Charles Wesley's poetry and prose." I have learned so much from many colleagues and friends who have been part of this scholarly fellowship over the years. In this regard I am particularly thankful for Tom Albin, Frank Baker, S T Kimbrough Jr., John Tyson, Dick Watson, and Carlton "Sam" Young. To these and to all those unnamed who have contributed to my knowledge and love of Charles Wesley, I gratefully dedicate this volume. I express my appreciation as well to my friend Andy Kinsey, who carefully and skillfully crafted the questions for consideration that make this resource more useful to the reader. I would not have been able to complete my work on this book had it not been for a study leave graciously approved by the president, John Shultz, and the trustees of Ashland Theological Seminary, to whom I offer my word of thanks. The ability to immerse myself in the poetry and prose of Charles Wesley without the distractions of administrative and faculty responsibilities has brought me great joy. My family, more than any others, continue to put a song in my heart, and the great poet-theologian of the church—Charles Wesley—continues to remind us that we never do anything alone in life:

> Help us to build each other up,
>   Our meager gifts improve,
> Increase our faith, confirm our hope,
>   And perfect us in love. (*HSP 1742*, 83)

Introduction

CHARLES WESLEY (1707–88), ONE of the most prolific hymn writers of all time, cofounded the Methodist movement with his older brother, John. Like his brother, he felt called by God to catalyze evangelical and sacramental renewal in the church. Charles, in fact, frequently led the way in many of the personal and institutional developments that characterized the religious awakening in eighteenth-century Britain. He founded the so-called Holy Club while a student at Oxford and experienced God's unconditional love in a spiritual transformation on May 21, 1738, that preceded the famous Aldersgate experience of John three days later. His primary gift that extends to global Christianity to this day was the production of some nine thousand hymns and sacred poems. It is not too much to say that Methodism was born in song; the early Methodists learned their theology primarily by singing Charles's hymns. In the early years of the revival it was not uncommon for Wesley to preach in the open air to a spellbound crowd gathered by his rich voice singing one of his own hymns. Found today in hymnals across the world of every imaginable variety, these hymns have also been a winsome expression of Christian ecumenism.

What kind of theologian was Charles Wesley and what is the unique contribution he makes to Wesleyan doctrine?[1] J. Ernest Rattenbury, perhaps the most significant student of the Wesley corpus during the first half of the twentieth century, described

1. The following observations parallel Chilcote, "Charles Wesley's Lyrical Credo."

Charles as an "experimental theologian." In his monumental study *The Evangelical Doctrines of Charles Wesley's Hymns*, in particular, he developed a portrait of his subject in a spirit very similar to that of Albert Outler's depiction of John Wesley as a "folk theologian." Rather than a "formal theologian," in the conventional sense of that term, Charles functioned as a popular theologian who oriented his theological work around the needs of the common person of his day. Somewhat in contrast to Rattenbury's positive evaluation, in his address entitled "Charles Wesley as Theologian" at the inaugural meeting of The Charles Wesley Society, Tom Langford subordinated the younger brother's theological role in the Wesleyan revival to that of John. He viewed Charles as "a theologian in the same sense that anyone who thinks, sings, paints, or dances about God is a theologian."[2] He was at best, in Langford's view, a "practical theologian," but of less immediate influence or abiding significance in matters of proper theology.

Langford was not unaware of Teresa Berger's ground-breaking dissertation published just a year prior to the conference, but the two scholars differed in their conclusions.[3] Berger argued that Wesley was a "doxological theologian," whose theological statements *to* God were of equal value to the theological affirmations of formal theologians *about* God. Unlike Langford, she viewed Wesley as a creative, first-order theologian whose hymns were theological documents of critical importance in the development of the Wesleyan theological heritage. Similarly, in his re-examination of Rattenbury's work on Charles, Brian Beck affirmed the theological weight of Charles's hymns. "We deceive ourselves," he maintained, "if we imagine that John Wesley's extensive theological writings were the decisive influence in the formation of the Methodist preachers or their hearers"; rather, the words that lingered in the hearts and minds of the Methodists were those of Charles's hymns.[4]

2. Langford, "Charles Wesley as Theologian," 99.

3. See Berger, *Theology in Hymns?*, the English translation of the dissertation.

4. Beck, "Rattenbury Revisited," 72.

Resonating strongly with Berger and Beck, Ted Campbell characterizes Wesley as *theologos*. He employs this Greek term to signify the importance of those who provide words (*logoi*) about God (*theos*). This description, Campbell argues, "allows us to claim more explicitly Charles Wesley's first-order work (*theologia prima*) of giving us words by which we can speak of God and indeed by which we can speak to God."[5] Also affirming the importance of Wesley as a theologian, John Tyson prefers to describe him as a "praxis theologian" since his fundamental concern was how Christian theology is lived out in the world.[6] Because of the work of these and other scholars, one can sense the development of a growing appreciation for Charles's theological significance today. In addition to the descriptions of Charles as experimental, practical, doxological, praxis theologian and as *theologos*, perhaps the most important characterization is that of Wesley as "lyrical theologian."[7]

In 1984, S T Kimbrough Jr. coined this term in reference to Charles. He aligns this description with other recent and important theological developments. In the current conversation between theology and the arts, for example, contemporary theologians like Jeremy Begbie have expanded the vision of a *theologia poetica*, including the relationship between sacred song and theology.[8] He maintains that poetry expresses theology potently, but also announces and performs faith in a different voice. He argues the ancient conviction that art, in its multifarious forms, must be recognized as a genuine theological text. A close connection abides between *theologia poetica* and *theologia lyrica*. In *The Lyrical Theology of Charles Wesley*, Kimbrough refines the concept, defining it as "a theology couched in poetry, song, and liturgy, characterized by rhythm and expressive of emotion and sentiment."[9] He explores

---

5. Campbell, "Charles Wesley, *Theologos*," 265.
6. See Tyson, "Theology of Charles Wesley's Hymns," 58–60.
7. See Chilcote, "Faith That Sings," 148–50.
8. See Begbie, *Resounding Truth*.
9. Kimbrough, *Lyrical Theology*, 3.

lyrical theology as both doxology and reflection—as both words to God and words about God.

Charles expressed the doxological dimension of his theology primarily in hymns composed for the purpose of worship and devotion. In these texts, according to Kimbrough, "he was seeking a continual offering of the human heart and life to God. Hence, the lyrical theology of doxology is multifaceted, multidimensional, and filled with diverse themes."[10] But other hymns demonstrate "his way of working through theological issues, thought, and concepts, and of shaping theological ideas" through a poetic medium.[11] Charles used hymns to reflect on the discursive theology of his brother and other theologians of the church. His eucharistic hymns illustrate this poignantly, as do his lyrical reflections on the meaning of significant historical events during his life, including the death of beloved friends. Through his poetic texts, Wesley created "a vibrant, lyrical theological memory individually and corporately for Christians and the church as a whole."[12]

The year 1739 marked Charles's entry into this distinctive role as lyrical theologian with the advent of three successive editions of *Hymns and Sacred Poems*, jointly published with his brother.[13] He published a fourth collection of this title in two volumes on his own in 1749 on the threshold of his marriage to Sarah Gwynne. Free from the editorial influence of his brother, this collection reveals some of Charles's unique theological concerns and perspectives. During his lifetime Charles also produced hymn collections on various themes, including the great festivals of the Christian year, the Trinity, families, times of trouble, and important theological topics such as "God's everlasting love." His 166 *Hymns on the Lord's Supper*, also a joint venture with John, demonstrate the centrality of the Eucharist to Methodist spirituality. In 1762 Wesley complet-

10. Ibid., 53.

11. Ibid., 54.

12. Ibid., 72.

13. On the complex relationship between the brothers and the attempt to "sort out" their respective theological commitments, see Newton, "Brothers in Arms."

ed a monumental project, a lyrical commentary on the entirety of scripture. Comprised of 2,349 sacred poems, this *Scripture Hymns* collection constitutes a poetic commentary on scripture unlike any other.[14] Scripture, in fact, pervades all the hymns of Charles Wesley. Rattenbury once claimed that if scripture were ever lost, it could be reconstituted through Charles's hymns. Wesley addresses nearly every conceivable doctrine within the sphere of Christian theology and his poetic corpus constitutes, therefore, a lyrical theology second to none in the English language.

Producing about 180 hymns per year from 1739 until his death in 1788, Wesley's most important publication was *A Collection of Hymns for the Use of the People Called Methodists*, published in 1780 with John. The editors' preface to the definitive edition of this "hymnbook," volume 7 of The Works of John Wesley, describes its significance with regard to Wesleyan doctrine:

> The *Sermons*—the *Notes*—the *Hymns*. These are the standard books of Wesleyan doctrine. Only the *Sermons* and *Notes* are "official" documents, but it is highly doubtful whether without the *Hymns* there could have been a Methodist revival. . . . The *Collection* was devoted to "directions for making our calling and election sure, for perfecting holiness in the fear of God," and the whole accent lies on "scriptural Christianity." The Bible, the whole Bible, nothing but the Bible—this is the theme of John Wesley's preaching and the glory of Charles's hymns.[15]

John Wesley, in his own preface to the *Collection*, described it as "a little body of experimental and practical divinity." One could find no better starting place for an exploration of Wesleyan doctrine than this collection of hymns. The conclusion of the editors concerning this body of lyrical theology, in fact, provided the impetus for this contribution to the Wesleyan Doctrine Series: "A summary list of key texts recurring throughout the *Collection* would serve as a basis for the *summa* of Charles Wesley's theology."[16]

14. See Kimbrough, "Charles Wesley's Lyrical Commentary."

15. Hildebrandt and Beckerlegge, introduction to the *Collection*, 1, 3.

16. Ibid., 5.

Rather than determining the contours of Wesley's theology on the basis of a broad study of his entire hymn corpus and other publications—an exercise too monumental for the scope of this book—I simply followed this recommendation. After examining the allusions to biblical texts in the hymns of the *Collection*, it was not difficult to identify the predominant biblical themes associated with these sources.[17] Entering into this process with a strong background in Wesleyan theology, I was pleasingly surprised by the results. The themes that emerged on the basis of this methodology reflect most of the prominent emphases of Wesleyan theology in general: a focus on christological concerns, the centrality of the doctrine of salvation, the importance of the means of grace, and the mandate of God's kingdom or rule. Charles brings his own unique personality, training, experience, and vision to bear, however, on these broad themes in the landscape of Christian doctrine. Nine chapters explore these themes.

The first two chapters examine who Jesus Christ was and is (the person of Christ) and what he did (the work of Christ). While Charles was a profoundly Trinitarian theologian, his theology also has a very strong christological focus. His doctrinal emphases revolve around Jesus. The next three chapters explore the Wesleyan *via salutis* (way of salvation). John Wesley identified what he considered to be *his* most central doctrines: "Our main doctrines which include all the rest are three, that of repentance, of faith, and of holiness. The first of these we account, as it were, the porch of religion; the next, the door; the third, religion itself."[18] The biblical themes in Charles's understanding of salvation follow exactly the same pattern. Chapter 3, therefore, articulates Charles's view of repentance and the necessity of a contrite heart. In chapter

---

17. The set of biblical verses (pericope) to which Wesley alludes most frequently in the *Collection* is Phil 2:1–11 (41 references); Phil 2:5 surfaces in the hymns 19 times. The individual verse referred to most frequently is Ezek 11:19 (22 references). Some of the other single verses or pericopes that figure most prominently in the hymns are 1 John 4:16–18 (28); Matt 6:8–13 (25); 2 Cor 3:14–18 (24); 1 Tim 1:15 (15); Matt 6:10 (13); 1 John 4:18 (13); and 1 Thess 5:17 (13), all of which function as "signature texts" in this volume.

18. Telford, *Letters of John Wesley*, 2:268.

4 we explore the interrelationship between God's grace and living faith in Wesley's conception of justification. Chapter 5 examines the process by which the Spirit restores the image of Christ in the believer through a process of sanctification leading to holiness of heart and life.

Wesley emphasizes growth in grace—the necessary corollary to his concept of salvation. The "means of grace" figure prominently, therefore, in his lyrical theology as spiritual instruments that establish and nourish a vital relationship with God. Chapter 6 describes his doctrine of prayer and the place of prayer in the Christian journey. Charles viewed the sacrament of the Lord's Supper, Eucharist, or Holy Communion as the "chief means of grace." Chapter 7 discusses the way in which the community of faith gathers around the table to be nourished spiritually and shaped into a loving people. In Charles's understanding of Christian discipleship, the follower of Jesus moves from the table into the world in mission. As in Jesus's own life and ministry, Charles's vision of the *missio Dei* (the mission of God) revolves around God's kingdom. Chapter 8 reflects the importance of this theme in Charles's theology and his call upon all Christians to live as ambassadors of reconciliation and shalom under God's rule. This study concludes with a final chapter devoted to Charles's unique vision of Christian perfection, or perfect love, the flying goal of the reclaimed and restored child of God.

A signature biblical text, one of those most frequently alluded to in the *Collection* as noted above, and a signature hymn text or sacred poem, provide foci in each chapter for an exploration of the respective biblical themes.[19] Charles weaves a golden thread throughout all his hymns, a cohesive element that holds all his doctrines together. His theology is a theology of grace upon grace.

19. All hymn texts throughout this study cite Wesley's first editions accessed through the website of the Center for Studies in the Wesleyan Tradition, Duke Divinity School: http://divinity.duke.edu/initiatives/cswt. Abbreviations for the various collections cited can be found in the bibliography, and numbers in parenthetical citations refer to the page numbers in the original edition, unless otherwise noted. Some texts have been slightly modernized for the benefit of the contemporary reader.

And for Charles, grace equals love. The task of the theologian—the task of all Christians—is to explore this central and universal truth, to submit to its transforming power, and to live it out in this world. For Charles all doctrine reflects a prayerful heart in quest of love:

> To love is all my wish,
> I only live for this:
> Grant me, Lord, my heart's desire,
>   There by faith forever dwell:
> This I always will require
>   Thee and only thee to feel.
>
> Thy power I pant to prove
> Rooted and fixed in love,
> Strengthened by thy Spirit's might,
>   Wise to fathom things divine,
> What the length and breadth and height,
>   What the depth of love like thine.
>
> Ah! Give me this to know
> With all thy saints below.
> Swells my soul to compass thee,
>   Gasps in thee to live and move,
> Filled with all the deity,
>   All immersed and lost in love! (*HSP 1739*, 169)

Questions for Consideration

1. What hymns and sacred songs come immediately to mind when speaking of the work of Charles Wesley?

2. What does the output of hymns and poetry by Charles Wesley say about the gifts he brought to the Wesleyan revivals and awakenings of the eighteenth century? Is there a sense that Charles's gifts have been overshadowed by his brother John's influence? How would the distinctive features of the Wesleyan revival have been different without Charles's input to devotion and song? What would have been lost?

3. In what ways is the description "lyrical theologian" helpful to characterize the theology of Charles Wesley? What other descriptions are there?

4. How might Wesley's "lyrical theology" fare and compare to the more contemporary hymns and songs in churches today? What theological themes and issues in Wesley's songs are still prevalent? What themes and issues are absent in today's contemporary expressions?

5. What is the "cohesive element" that runs through the hymns of Charles Wesley, holding them together? Explain.

one

Incarnation: The Word Became Flesh

EVERYTHING IN CHARLES WESLEY'S lyrical theology revolves around the affirmation and worship of a Triune God of love, the God of truth and grace. He composed many hymns on the theme of the Trinity and published two collections devoted exclusively to this subject, the first in 1746 and the second in 1767. His concept of the Three-One God—Father, Son, and Holy Spirit—pervades both his poetry and his prose. He believed that people come to know this God not only through God's supreme self-revelation in the Word (Jesus Christ, the Second Person of the Trinity) but also in the word (scripture), the record of God's interaction with the world and the people God loves. He had a simple but profound vision of God and life with God: God is love; God created all that is as an extension of God's love. Scripture testifies to the fact that "God created humanity in God's own image, in the divine image God created them, male and female God created them" (Gen 1:27). God breathed human beings into existence, therefore, that they might receive love and share love with God and others.[1]

---

1. See an exceptional treatment of these themes in Kimbrough, "Charles Wesley and a Window to the East," 165–83.

Wesley celebrates the majestic nature of the Trinity, the God who creates, redeems, and sustains all life, in a lyrical creed published in 1747.

> Father, in whom we live,
>   In whom we are and move,
> The glory, power, and praise receive
>   Of thy creating love.
> Let all the angel-throng
>   Give thanks to God on high,
> While earth repeats the joyful song,
>   And echoes to the sky.
>
> Incarnate deity,
>   Let all the ransomed race
> Render in thanks their lives to thee
>   For thy redeeming grace;
> The grace to sinners showed,
>   Ye heavenly choirs proclaim,
> And cry Salvation to our God,
>   Salvation to the Lamb.
>
> Spirit of holiness,
>   Let all thy saints adore
> Thy sacred energy, and bless
>   Thine heart-renewing power
> Not angel-tongues can tell
>   Thy love's ecstatic height,
> The glorious joy unspeakable,
>   The beatific sight.
>
> Eternal Triune Lord,
>   Let all the hosts above,
> Let all the sons of men record,
>   And dwell upon thy love;

> When heaven and earth are fled
>> Before thy glorious face,
> Sing all the saints thy love hath made,
>> Thine everlasting praise. (*Redemption Hymns*, 44–45)

This doxological "hymn to the Trinity" elevates each Person of the Trinity in turn through the successive stanzas before concluding with the singers' response in praise, gratitude, and adoration.[2] Charles's hymn, as S T Kimbrough has observed, puts worship at the center of life, makes life itself an act of praise, trusts in the sacred energy of God, and focuses all on God's self-giving love.[3]

Wesley locates the very meaning of our existence in this understanding of God; God created humanity to celebrate the love of the Creator, to embrace the love we see in Jesus as our way of life, and to permit the Spirit to restore the image of this God in our lives. The original image of God stamped upon us in creation, and then lost in the fall, anticipates a return to perfection as the goal of life. Seeking to love as God loves defines authentic human existence. This knowledge of God, the meaning of life, and the purpose of existence only becomes real or visible, in Charles's view, as we see the one, true God in the face of Jesus. Otherwise, God remains unknown, as one of his *Nativity Hymns* (1745) makes abundantly clear.

> God the invisible *appears*,
>> God the blest, the great I AM
> Sojourns in this vale of tears,
>> And Jesus is his name. (6)

The incarnation, therefore, plays a central role in Charles Wesley's theology. It is the first biblical theme in his theology that we will explore together.

2. See Yrigoyen, *Praising the God of Grace*, 13–24.
3. Kimbrough, *Heart to Praise My God*, 135.

The Nature of Incarnation

When "the Word became flesh and lived among us," he revealed the true nature and glory of God. In a hymn on "the presence of the Lord," based on Matthew 1:23, Wesley affirms this central fact about Immanuel ("God with us"):

> Celebrate Immanuel's name,
>   The Prince of life and peace!
> God with us our lips proclaim,
>   Our faithful hearts confess:
> God is in our flesh revealed,
>   Earth and heaven in Jesus join,
> Mortal with Immortal filled,
>   And human with Divine.
>
> Fullness of the Deity
>   In Jesus' body dwells,
> Dwells in all his saints and me,
>   When God his Son reveals:
> Father, manifest thy Son,
>   And conscious of the incarnate Word
> In our inmost souls make known
>   The Presence of the Lord. (MS Matthew, 4)

God's self-disclosure, as it were, climaxes in the wonderful yet inscrutable birth of Jesus and all that follows from it, including the suffering, death, resurrection, and ascension of Christ. Though faith, as we shall see, is much more than the affirmation of this spiritual truth, this mystery touches on every aspect of Christian faith and life.

Rather than attempting to explain the incarnation in philosophical terms as if to master the inexplicable, Wesley simply describes the lengths to which God's love will go to reach people wherever they are. God "emptied himself of all but love," he sings, "and died to ransom *me!*" (MS Hymns OT, 29). The ramifications of this divine self-emptying stagger the mind. God becomes a human being so that those redeemed through Christ might become one with God. Christ empties himself of glory and eternity, of every divine attribute save one, the essence of God, which is love. Fully divine—all love and nothing but love—he enters our world of brokenness and sin, takes on a human nature, and makes it possible for God to incarnate love in others. Like many of the earliest theologians of the church, in other words, Charles used *kenosis*—self-emptying—as a metaphor to more fully understand the nature of God's mysterious act of incarnation.

A Kenotic Paradigm

Charles viewed God's self-emptying, self-limitation, and self-effacement in the incarnation of Jesus Christ as the primary building blocks of Christian theology and spirituality. He drew these images primarily from St. Paul's Letter to the Philippians, in which the apostle reminded the community to imitate the Christ of whom they sang in one of the earliest hymns of the church:

> Let the same mind be in you that was in Christ Jesus, who, though he was in the form of God, did not regard equality with God as something to be exploited, but emptied himself, taking the form of a slave, being born in human likeness. And being found in human form, he humbled himself and became obedient to death—even death on a cross. Therefore God also highly exalted him and gave him the name that is above every name, so that at the name of Jesus every knee should bend, in heaven and on earth and under the earth, and every tongue should confess that Jesus Christ is Lord, to the glory of God the Father. (2:5–11)

This *kenotic* hymn, in fact, figures prominently in Charles's sacred poetry and functions as the signature biblical text to frame the theme of this chapter.[4] For him, how does this *kenotic* imagery function as both a way to understand the mystery of the

---

4. See Kimbrough, "*Kenosis* in the Nativity Hymns," 262–85.

incarnation and as a paradigm for faithful Christian discipleship, since the two are intimately connected?

Wesley reflects on St. Paul's use of this ancient hymn in a twenty-stanza lyrical paraphrase of "Let this mind be in you, which was also in Christ Jesus" (Phil 2:5). It describes the mind of Christ in each successive stanza as quiet, gentle, patient, noble, spotless, loving, thankful, constant, and perfect. His most profound exposition of the *kenotic* theme comes in an extremely significant hymn in which he explores the titles of Christ. This sacred poem could easily be described as the signature hymn for the incarnational theme in his theology:

> Arise, my soul, arise,
> Thy Savior's sacrifice!
> All the names that love could find,
> All the forms that love could take,
> Jesus in himself has joined,
> Thee, my soul, his own to make.

> Equal with God most high,
> He laid his glory by:
> He the eternal God was born,
> Man with men he deigned to appear,
> Object of his creature's scorn,
> Pleased a servant's form to wear.

> High above every name,
> Jesus, the great I AM!
> Bows to Jesus every knee,
> Things in heaven, and earth, and hell;
> Saints adore him, demons flee,
> Fiends, and men, and angels feel.

> He left his throne above,
> Emptied of all but love:

Whom the heavens cannot contain,
God vouchsafed a worm to appear,
Lord of glory, Son of man,
Poor, and vile, and abject here. (*HSP 1739*, 165–67)

Two primary and interrelated themes in Wesley's *kenotic* paradigm emerge from this hymn, namely, humility and self-emptying.

Humility and Self-Emptying

These ideas are distinct, but inseparable. In the incarnation God literally humbles God's self to the dust. Wesley provides here a portrait of a God who "laid his glory by"—the Eternal entering into time and space—or as elsewhere he exclaims in wonder, "God contracted to a span." The incarnation comes to full poetic expression, as one may well expect, in Charles's *Nativity Hymns* (1745), which celebrate Jesus's birth. The opening stanzas of one hymn in particular (Hymn 15) articulate the mystery of the incarnation with exceptional potency:

All-wise, all-good, Almighty Lord,
Jesus, by highest heaven adored,
  Ere time its course began,
How did your glorious mercy stoop
To take the fallen nature up,
  When you became a man?

The eternal God from heaven came down,
The King of Glory dropped his crown,
  And veiled his majesty,
Emptied of all but love he came;
Jesus, I call you by your name
  Your pity bore for me. (*Nativity Hymns*, 19)

In both of these stanzas Charles uses the images of "stooping," "dropping," and even "emptying" to describe the character of God.

In the incarnation, in other words, God relinquished all those characteristics we generally associate with the divine —omnipotence, omniscience, omnipresence—without compromising the core essence of the divine nature, namely, love. God, in the Second Person of the Trinity, comes down to the human level, enters into this world, and demonstrates the lengths to which love will go to establish and nurture relationships of love. The true God desires union with all humanity. The purpose of creation was to celebrate relationships of love. God seeks the restoration of this goal above all things. The essence of the paradox—the key to the mystery of love—is self-emptying, and we find this concept everywhere in Charles's poetry. In his *Hymns on the Lord's Supper* (1745) the singer confesses, "He came self-emptied from above, / That we might live through him" (44). In a lyrical paraphrase of Luke 2:19 Wesley ponders the miraculous nature of Jesus's birth with Mary, his mother:

> Emptied of all his majesty:
> O may I always bear in mind
> The Savior's pity for mankind,
> Which brought Him from His throne,
> Emptied of all His majesty,
> A Man of griefs to comfort me,
> And make my heart His own. (MS Luke, 28)

In his famous hymn entitled "Free Grace" and more popularly known by the opening line, "And can it be, that I should gain," he condenses the whole *kenotic* doctrine, as elsewhere, into that single line:

> He left his Father's throne above
>   (So free, so infinite his grace!),
> *Emptied himself of all but love,*
>   And bled for Adam's helpless race.
> 'Tis mercy all, immense and free,
> For, O my God, it found out me.
> (*HSP 1739*, 118; italics added)

The God who created all that exists takes on flesh and enters human history. The uncreated Word, one with the Creator before time began, begins to be. He who is Alpha and Omega, the beginning and the end, from everlasting to everlasting, comes into this world at a particular time, in a particular place, to a particular human family. The infinite, almighty God becomes a finite human creature. The Second Person of the Trinity, who is God from God and Light from Light—immortal, invisible, God only wise—becomes transparent in the son of a Galilean carpenter. The face of this child reveals the true character of God. What shines through? Jesus reveals the truth of holiness and the truth of blessedness. He provides a portrait of a human life as God truly intends it to be lived. The vision transforms others. Once those who knew Jesus saw God in his face, they could never be the same again. This gift filled the souls of his followers with a genuine blessedness that overflowed and took full possession of their hearts. They stood in awe of the love exhibited by Jesus in his earthly life and knew that this Jesus was their all in all—the goal of their living, the fullest happiness they could seek, the reason for their very existence. His face was full of grace and truth.

Full of Grace and Truth

In the 525 hymns of the *Collection* Charles alludes to John 1:14—"And the Word became flesh and lived among us, and we have seen his glory, the glory as of a father's only son, full of grace and truth"—more than any other Gospel text. More often than not, the allusion is to that concluding phrase. He built his theology of the incarnation on the foundation of grace. As was true for his older brother, John, grace provided the two grand heads of doctrine. Grace pertains, first of all, to the work of God *for us* in Jesus Christ. But Charles also defined grace in relation to the work of God *in us* through the power of the Holy Spirit. He establishes a direct connection between this grace and the loving God known to us as Father, Son, and Holy Spirit. The incarnate Christ reveals a grace-defined God. Charles conceives this grace primarily in terms of loving relationships. So he often uses the terms *grace* and *love* interchangeably. The word *grace* embraces the full image of God, creation, and humankind. This expansive understanding of love and grace inevitably links theology and practice. Wesley finds it impossible to separate thoughts about God from actions in relation to God; God's gracious love holds everything together and gives meaning and purpose to all created things.

It is not uncommon, therefore, for Charles to express his understanding of the Christian life as a pilgrimage of "grace upon grace." All life moves from God to God, and the pilgrim makes this journey in Christ—in the incarnate God. A vision of the Christian faith that is rooted in a Wesleyan doctrine of God begins in grace, grows in grace, and finds its ultimate completion in grace. God's grace, or unmerited love, restores relationships with God and others and renews God's own image in the lives of the beloved. Through grace, God leads all creation into a dance of joy, justice, and jubilee in which God's beloved children seek to radiate God's love, participate in God's reign, and desire the restoration of all things in the Three-One God. The necessary corollary of the incarnation is Christian discipleship, understood primarily as a grace-filled response to the free gift of God's all-sufficient grace. For Wesley "talk about God" leads seamlessly into "talk about life," especially as it is lived out in Christ through the power of the Spirit.

In his hymns, Charles demonstrates the importance of this gracious character of God extended to every person and manifest so richly in the incarnation. He frequently collapses the phrase "full of truth and grace" into the simplified "full of grace" for its lyrical use. The first hymn in which this phrase appears in the *Collection* comes in the section "Describing the Goodness of God." Charles refers to it there as God's "kindest word" and associates it with the "arms of mercy." Indeed, Charles associates this image of embrace perennially with the concept of God's grace:

> O Jesu, full of pardoning grace,
>> More full of grace than I of sin;
> Yet once again I seek thy face.
>> Open thine arms and take me in. (*HSP 1749*, 1:158)

Wherever he uses this phrase he consistently paints a portrait of a God who "is only love," who desires the restoration of all, who seeks to lift up all people, whose "love can find a thousand ways." The incarnation of grace and truth in Christ elicits a heartfelt prayer:

> Come, thou high and lofty Lord,
> Lowly, meek, incarnate Word,
> Humbly stoop to earth again,
> Come, and visit abject man. (*HSP 1740*, 182)

In these expressions of lyrical theology, Wesley describes the Three-One God as the friend of humanity. In Jesus Christ, God enters human history, comes close, and offers friendship to every person. Wesley never wavered from this central conviction that the act of the incarnation reveals the character of God's transforming grace, friendship, and love. Wesley's explication of the incarnation, therefore, leads directly to a concrete human response. Having encountered God's unconditional love in Jesus, those touched and transformed by his grace become the instruments of that same love in the world. Faith in Jesus entails both gift and responsibility. All these themes coalesce in Charles's amazing lyrical paraphrase of the Gospel text, John 1:14:

> What angel can the grace explain!
> The very God is very man,
>   By love paternal given!
> Begins the uncreated Word,
> Born is the everlasting Lord,
>   Who made both earth and heaven!
>
> Behold him high above all height,
> Him, God of God, and Light of Light
>   In a mean earthy shrine;
> Jehovah's glory dwelt with men,
> The Person in our flesh is seen,
>   The character divine!

Not with these eyes of flesh and blood;
Yet lo, we still behold the God
  Replete with truth and grace:
The truth of holiness we see,
The truth of full felicity
  In our Redeemer's face.

Transformed by the ecstatic sight,
Our souls o'erflow with pure delight,
  And every moment own
The Lord our whole perfection is,
The Lord is our immortal bliss,
  And Christ and heaven are one. (*Scripture Hymns*, 2:239–40)

Through the incarnation, then, God demonstrates in an irrefutable manner that God is merciful and gracious, slow to anger, and abounding in steadfast love and faithfulness (Exod 34:6). The God of the Hebrew Scriptures is the same God made visible in the face of Jesus. In another hymn on this text, Charles celebrates this God of pure, unbounded love and grace. He describes that love as ceaseless and unexhausted, unmerited and free, faithful and constant, unalterably sure. Likewise, God's truth and goodness are unfathomable and plenteous. This God delights, helps, waits, saves. Moreover, the full energy of God's love and grace extends to every creature: "enough for all, enough for each, / enough for evermore" (*Scripture Hymns*, 1:53). By this use of language, Charles demonstrates the intimate connection between creation and redemption. God does not do something different in sending the Son as Redeemer and Lord. God has always radiated light throughout the universe—always extends God's very self to all in love. The love that spoke this universe into being is the same Word that came to dwell among us in the flesh, in the person of Jesus of Nazareth, to heal and restore. In the beginning, God said, "Let light shine"; in the middle, the Radiance of God—Christ our Lord—shines in the hearts of the faithful; at the end, all shall be lost, as Charles sings, in the glory of this Light. Wesley poured all his energy into the proclamation of this good news about the incarnate One who is prophet, priest, and king.

The Threefold Office of Christ

God not only entered human history in the Second Person of the Trinity to reveal the nature of God's love for all and to all. The incarnate God lived out that love in the midst of human uncertainty, struggle, and brokenness. Charles connected his conception of the person of Christ in an integral manner with the work of Christ in this world in the context of his earthly ministry and mission. His understanding of Christ, in this regard, drew upon a long-standing tradition in Western theology. He understood Jesus's life and work through the lens of his offices as prophet, priest, and king.[5] And this threefold office of Christ sets the backdrop for the doctrine of redemption, which we will explore in the next chapter. These offices not only reveal more fully who Jesus was and is but also help us understand who we are in relation to this God of love.

Christ's role as priest precedes his other work of restoration. No one ever outgrows his or her need of Christ as priest. All receive God's pardon through his priestly office. But God not only offers forgiveness; God delivers from the power of sin those who trust in Christ. As prophet, Christ reveals the moral image that God intends for everyone. Christ restores an awareness of God's law and initiates the renewal of Christlike character. Christ the king leads all potentially toward that full recovery. The present work of Christ comes to its full fruition, then, through the office of Christ as king. Christ as Lord rules in all believing hearts and enables full conformity to his own image as the believer grows into the fullest possible love of God and neighbor. Christ not only saves through dying on the cross and thereby procuring our forgiveness; Christ's redemptive work also includes growth in holiness of heart and life. Christ as priest forgives; Christ as prophet guides; Christ as king restores. So from this exploration of the person of Christ, we turn

5. See Tyson's helpful discussion of the offices in *Charles Wesley*, 40–41.

our attention to the redemptive work of Christ—a second biblical theme in the lyrical theology of Charles Wesley.

Questions for Consideration

1. What is the central theological affirmation around which Charles Wesley's hymns revolve?

2. How does the signature poem "Arise, my soul, arise" speak to the relationship of the incarnation and the *kenotic* theme of Christ's self-emptying?

3. How does Charles relate but keep distinct the themes of humility and self-emptying when describing the incarnation? How does the phrase "God contracted to a span" help express God becoming human?

4. How do the images of "stooping," "dropping," and "emptying" help describe the character of God?

5. How do the biblical texts of John 1:14 and Philippians 2:5–11 play into the lyrical theology of Charles Wesley and the doctrine of grace as God working *for us* and *in us*?

6. How does "talk about God" lead inevitably to "talk about life"? In other words, what is the relationship between the incarnation and discipleship?

7. What is the threefold office of Christ? What is the relationship of the offices to the Trinity? How is this relationship to be lived out in faithful service?

two

Redemption: The Lamb That Was Slain

CHARLES WESLEY INTIMATELY RELATES his doctrine of the incarnation to the primary purpose of God coming in the flesh—the atonement of all and reconciliation with God. In the first chapter we explored Wesley's understanding of the incarnation and the way in which this act of God shapes the Christian vision of God and life in Christ. To use the more classical theological category, we examined essentially his understanding of the "person of Christ." In this chapter we will reflect upon how Charles expounds the "work of Christ." The first two doctrines or themes in this study, therefore, revolve around the two central christological concerns—who Jesus Christ was and what he did. "Incarnation and atonement," as John Tyson has observed, "dominated [Wesley's] hymnological landscape."[1] The redemptive work of Christ—atonement—plays a role equal to that of incarnation in Wesley's theology.[2]

1. Tyson, *Charles Wesley*, 40.

2. D. M. Baillie, in his monumental postwar study entitled *God Was in Christ*, demonstrates the centrality of Christology to all aspects of Christian theology and the necessity of holding together the Jesus of history and the Christ of faith, the person of Christ and his work, incarnation and atonement.

In a hymn entitled "Desiring to Love" Charles articulates well his multidimensional view of the redemptive work of Christ:

> What shall I do my God to love,
>   My Savior, and the world's to praise?
> Whose mercy and compassion move
>   To me, and all the fallen race;
> Whose mercy is divinely free
> For all the fallen race, and me.
>
> I long to know, and to make known
>   The height and depth of love divine,
> The kindness thou to me hast shown,
>   Whose every sin was counted thine:
> My God for me resigned his breath,
> He died, to save my soul from death.
>
> All souls are thine: and thou for all
>   The ransom of thy life hast given,
> To raise the sinner from his fall,
>   And bring him back to God and heaven,
> Thou all the world hast died to save,
> And all may thy salvation have. (*HSP 1742*, 24–25)

Jesus came to save, and Charles demonstrates his belief that those who seek God receive redemption in a manner unique and appropriate to them; no single theory of atonement suffices for him. His doctrine of the redemptive work of Christ is richly textured, reflecting all the classical theories drawn from various strands of the biblical witness. His reference to Christ taking the sin of humanity upon himself sounds very much like a substitutionary or satisfaction theory of atonement. His theology reflects a deep concern for the effects of sin and the brokenness that characterizes all people. His conception of Christ's victory over death reflects a more ancient *Christus Victor*—Christ the victor—theme, as does his reference to the metaphor of ransom and release. Drawing images primarily from the Apostle Paul, his vision of redemption entails our victory through Christ over all those powers that separate us from God's love and God's loving ways, particularly sin, death, and evil. He alludes to the moral influence theory of atonement in his explication of "love divine" and its implied power to transform. According to Charles, God must find some way to turn human beings around and thereby fix their attention on what really matters in life. Nothing has greater transformative power than the revelation of God's love in the self-sacrifice of Jesus on the cross where Jesus gives his life for his friends. As in many other areas of his theology, Wesley reveals a synthetic approach that refuses a simplistic or reductionistic understanding of the ways of God.

He devoted an entire collection of hymns to the theme of redemption: *Hymns for those that seek, and those that have Redemption in the Blood of Jesus Christ* (1747). But his interest in explicating Jesus's redemptive work—an evangelistic desire for others to understand and embrace it—pervades Wesley's hymns and prose works. In the *Collection*, Charles alludes to 1 Timothy 1:15, "The saying is sure and worthy of full acceptance, that Christ Jesus came into the world to save sinners," no less than fifteen times. This signature text identifies the primary purpose of the incarnation. First and foremost for Charles, Jesus is the One who comes to save sinners. Another frequently quoted biblical text in his hymns, John 1:29, "Behold the Lamb of God, which taketh away the sin of the world," provides more texture to Wesley's fundamental understanding of the redemptive work of Christ by using a weighty title for Jesus. This Jesus, as he sings, is "the Lamb that was slain." The record of his preaching, moreover, reflects an amazing consistency on this point. He preached more sermons on John 1:36, "Behold the Lamb of God," than on any other text.[3]

In his *Scripture Hymns* Wesley provides a lyrical paraphrase of this particular confession of faith in John's Gospel. The hymn provides something of an outline for an examination of his doctrine of universal redemption:

3. See Tyson, *Charles Wesley*, 487.

Did Jesus for the world atone?
  "Yes; for the world of the elect:"
LOVE could not die for some alone,
  And all the wretched rest reject:
For the whole helpless world that lay
  In desperate wickedness, he died,
And all who dare believe it, may
  With me be freely justified.

Charged with the universal load,
  The sins of every soul, and mine,
By faith I see the Lamb of God,
  The bleeding sacrifice divine!
My sins, transferred from me to him,
  Shall never be by justice found,
All carried down that purple stream,
  All in that open fountain drowned! (2:241)

Charles is serious about the issue of human sin, that primary reality separating the human creature from the Creator. He provides multiple images with regard to the redemptive work of Christ—word pictures that revolve around classical biblical conceptions of purchase, pardon, purification, power, and prescription. He articulates a vision of universal redemption and interfaces the objective work of cross with the interior activity of the Holy Spirit.

The Problem of Sin

Sin alienates beloved children from their loving Creator.[4] Tyson elaborates on Wesley's view of sin and its relationship to redemption: "His theology of redemption was grounded in a rigorous affirmation of the reality of human sin, both in its original and

4. A discussion of redemption requires a brief examination of the sinful human condition, but we will examine sin and its consequences more fully in the successive chapters related to the way of salvation, and the next chapter on repentance, in particular.

actual aspects. He expressed this conviction about sin in colorful and dramatic imagery that was designed to strip off layers of pride and self-centeredness and to cast the reader or singer wholeheartedly upon Christ."[5] In his poetic descriptions of human sin Charles does not imply that everything a person does is evil, that there is no good in humanity whatsoever; rather, sin refers to the brokenness that touches every aspect of human life. The following excerpt reveals the crux of the matter, in Wesley's view:

> Thou art darkness in my mind,
>> Perverseness in my will,
> Love inordinate and blind,
>> Which always cleaves to ill. (*HSP 1742*, 235)

For Charles, sin is the absence of light, represented here by darkness and perversity. His poetic language of "love inordinate" is reminiscent of St. Augustine's view of "disordered affections" in the human being. The human problem is not an inability to love; rather, human beings simply love the wrong things in the wrong way. Instead of loving God as an end or ultimate goal, God's children love their Creator as a means to their own ends. As Augustine observed, only God can reorder human affections or loves and resituate the life of the wayward child on the right path.

Sin not only alienates the beloved from the Lover; sin encumbers the child of God, as Charles confesses in one of his most potent *Redemption Hymns*:

> Weary of this war within,
>> Weary of this endless strife,
> Weary of ourselves and sin,
>> Weary of a wretched life;
>
> . . . .
>
> Burdened with a world of grief,
>> Burdened with our sinful load,
> Burdened with this unbelief,
>> Burdened with the wrath of God. (12–13)

---

5. Tyson, *Charles Wesley on Sanctification*, 55.

God seeks to redeem this situation through an amazing act of love. One of Charles's favorite titles for Jesus, then, is "friend of sinners." He introduces this image in the very first stanza of his *Redemption Hymns* collection. "Jesus, my Lord, attend / Thy fallen creature's cry," the singer pleads, "And show thyself the sinner's friend" (1). When Jesus befriends sinners, and they, wearied and burdened, then open their hearts to a God of grace, that friendship liberates, heals, and restores. The dominant verbs of the full hymn reflect Charles's vision of redemption. Release. Forgive. Heal. Restore. Impute. Impart. Jesus—the sinner's friend—releases his friends from the oppressive power of evil, forgives their sin, and reconciles them with God.

Images of Redemption

It should not be surprising that so many of Charles's hymns touch on his theology of the cross in one way or another. Tyson has gone so far as to say that, not unlike Martin Luther, his *theologia crucis* "is a fundamental, integrating feature in his writings."[6] J. Ernest Rattenbury described one of the hymns Wesley published in *Hymns on the Lord's Supper* (1745) as a "Protestant crucifix."[7] The hymn is a lyrical depiction of Christ on the cross—an icon of the crucifixion:

> Endless scenes of wonder rise
>   With that mysterious tree,
> Crucified before our eyes
>   Where we our Maker see:
> Jesus, Lord, what hast thou done!
>   Publish we the death divine,
> Stop, and gaze, and fall, and own
>   Was never love like thine!

6. Tyson, "'I Preached at the Cross,'" 204.
7. See Rattenbury, *Eucharistic Hymns*, 20–30.

> Never love nor sorrow was
>   Like that my Jesus showed;
> See him stretched on yonder cross
>   And crushed beneath our load!
> Now discern the deity,
>   Now his heavenly birth declare!
> Faith cries out 'Tis he, 'tis he,
>   My God that suffers there! (16)

This servant image of the crucified Christ, reminiscent of the Servant Song images of Isaiah, reveals a God who attempts neither to coerce love nor to impose it. The redemptive work of this loving God, in Charles's view, requires a wide range of biblical images to expound it fully, and he employs them all. But the preeminent themes in his theology of the cross include Christ as sacrifice, Christ as victor, and Christ as healer.

Christ as Sacrifice

The following language sets the tone of Charles's sacrificial imagery as it relates to redemption:

> For what you have done
> His blood must atone:
> The Father hath punished for you his dear Son.
>   The Lord in the day
>   Of his anger did lay
> Your sins on the Lamb; and he bore them away.
> (HSP 1749, 1:87)

His sermon based on Romans 3:23–24 not only echoes the sentiments of this hymn but reflects Wesley's dependence on the Anglican Homily "Of Salvation" for his views: "God sent his only Son our Saviour Christ into this world, to fulfil the law for us, and by the shedding of his most precious blood, to make a sacrifice and satisfaction or amends to his Father for our sins, and assuage his wrath and indignation conceived against us for the same."[8] The idea of Christ as sacrifice derives primarily from the Letter to the Hebrews, in which the writer exploits this image more fully than any other New Testament author to explain the meaning of the cross. The concept of sacrifice, of course, reaches deep into the liturgical practice of the Hebrews (and virtually every religious tradition) as the primary means of understanding the reconciliation of alienated people to their covenant God.

In many of his *Redemption Hymns*, in fact, Charles explicitly connects sacrificial atonement in Jewish practice with the cross of the Messiah:

> O Lamb of God, to thee
> In deep distress I flee,
> Thou didst purge my guilty stain,
> Didst for all atonement make;
> Take away my sin and pain,
> Save me for thy mercy's sake. (33)

Christ's offering of himself on the cross atones for sin in one great sacrifice of love, once for all. In the successive stanzas of this hymn, as in all of Wesley's poetry, the verbs do the work and provide the power of his lyrical theology. Hasten. Purge. Tear away. Remove. Cast out. Charles's mystical flame surfaces in the imagery of this hymn: Flood me with thy cleansing tide. Plunge me in the crimson flood. Drown my sins in the Red Sea. Swallow up my soul in thee! No verb serves his purposes more effectively, however, than the verb "to shed." The penultimate stanza brings climax to the hymn as the Spirit of God applies the effects of Jesus's sacrifice to the child of God:

> This, this is all my plea,
> Thy blood was shed for me,
> Shed, to wash my conscience clean,
> Shed to purify my heart,
> Shed to purge me from all sin,

8. "Sermon 6: Romans 3:23–24," in Newport, *Sermons*, 171.

> Shed to make me as thou art. (34)

In this single hymn, despite his focus on the sacrificial imagery of redemption, Wesley elevates at least three aspects of God's work in refashioning the soul: (1) cleansing—Christ's blood was shed "to wash my conscience clean"; (2) purification—Christ's blood was shed "to purify my heart," "to purge me from all sin"; and (3) restoration—Christ's blood was shed "to make me as thou art." More important than anything else, for Charles, the sacrifice of Christ restores the capacity to love.[9]

Christ as Victor

Some have argued that the *Christus Victor* concept of redemption dominated the earliest Christian community and served as the primary theory of atonement during the church's first millennium. According to this tradition, often linked with the language of ransom, the cross both secures and signals the victory of Christ on the cross over the powers that hold humanity in bondage. The theme of victory over cosmic foes—over sin, death, and evil—pervades the New Testament. Charles picks up on these themes, which come to joyous expression in his hymns for Easter and Ascension, in particular. But no hymn celebrates this victory with greater power than "Jesus the conqueror reigns" (*HSP 1749*, 1:232–34). Various selections from this sixteen-stanza hymn must suffice.

> Jesus the conqueror reigns,
> In glorious strength arrayed,
> His kingdom over all maintains,
> And bids the earth be glad. (1:232)

As a consequence of the cross, "Our sins are washed away," claims Charles. "The guilt, the guilt of sin is gone." "Our mountain-sins melt down, and flow / And sink into his blood." Jesus also conquers the ultimate enemy. "Death is all swallowed down, / The

---

9. For an examination of the image of blood in Wesley's theology of redemption, see Tyson, *Charles Wesley on Sanctification*, 115–56.

power can never stay" (1:234). The great usurper of God's rule—
Satan—falls to the victorious power of Jesus's love:

> Satan shall be repelled;
> The world's imperious god
> Shall fly before our sacred shield,
> Our trust in Jesus' blood:
> Jesus hath cleft his crown,
> Of old from glory driven,
> And cast the bold aspirer down,
> As lightening out of Heaven. (1:233)

On the cross, Jesus champions the plight of the lost:

> Our advocate with God,
> He undertakes our cause,
> And spreads through all the earth abroad
> The victory of his cross. (1:232)

According to Charles, the conquest over sin, death, and evil
won through the cross continues in heaven as the risen Christ
intercedes eternally for all God's children. Charles develops this
theme in a hymn based on John 19:5, "Behold the man!" Synthetic
in nature, this lyrical celebration weaves together the language of
sacrifice, substitution, and purchase to describe the salvific nature
of Jesus's work on the cross, all within the larger context of Jesus's
victory:

> Arise, my soul, arise,
> Shake off thy guilty fears,
> The bleeding sacrifice
> In my behalf appears;
> Before the throne my surety stands;
> My name is written on his hands.
>
> He ever lives above
> For me to intercede,
> His all-redeeming love,

His precious blood to plead;
His blood atoned for all our race,
And sprinkles now the throne of grace.

Five bleeding wounds he bears,
    Received on Calvary;
They pour effectual prayers,
    They strongly speak for me;
Forgive him, O forgive, they cry,
Nor let that ransomed sinner die! (*HSP 1742*, 264–65)

Christ as Healer

Through the cross, the Great Physician also heals. "My spirit's desperate wound," Wesley acknowledges, "I cannot slightly heal" (*HSP 1749*, 1:108). God must do for the broken what they cannot do for themselves. Through the redemptive work of Christ, God applies a balm that makes the wounded whole. In an extended lyrical reflection on 1 Corinthians 10:11, "These things were written for our instruction," Charles expresses his deepest hope with regard to the work of grace:

From sin, the guilt, the power, the pain,
    Thou wilt redeem my soul.
Lord, I believe; and not in vain:
    My faith shall make me whole. (*HSP 1740*, 74)

Perhaps it is for this reason that allusions to Luke 7:22 and its synoptic counterparts figure so prominently in Charles's hymns—"tell John what things ye have seen and heard; how that the blind see, the lame walk, the lepers are cleansed, the deaf hear, the dead are raised, to the poor the gospel is preached."

Most of those familiar at all with the hymns of Charles Wesley identify this allusion immediately with one of his most famous hymns, "O for a thousand tongues to sing," in which the deaf hear, the tongues of the dumb are loosened, the blind see, and the lame leap for joy. But another hymn, "Sinners, believe the gospel-word," which functions as the signature hymn for the theme of redemption, locates all within the broader context of redemption.

> Sinners, believe the gospel-word,
>> Jesus is come, your souls to save!
> Jesus is come, your common Lord!
>> Pardon ye all in him may have;
> May now be saved, whoever will:
> This man receiveth sinners still.

> See where the lame, the halt, the blind,
>> The deaf, the dumb, the sick, the poor
> Flock to the friend of humankind,
>> And freely all accept their cure:
> To whom doth he his help deny?
> Whom in his days of flesh pass by?

> Did not his word, the fiends expel?
>> The lepers cleanse, and raise the dead?
> Did he not all their sickness heal,
>> And satisfy their every need?
> Did he reject his helpless clay,
> Or send them sorrowful away? (*Love Hymns 1741*, 21)

Universal Redemption

The entire collection from which this last hymn is taken rails against what Charles considered to be the unbiblical teachings of irresistible grace and the predestination of the elect. Some of his most polemical hymns were directed against those who sought to limit the range of God's redemptive work in Christ.[10] The most important issue for Charles in this controversy with the Calvinists

---

10. On the critical debate between Charles and his Calvinistic detractors, see Wainwright, "Charles Wesley and Calvinism," 184–203.

can be formulated as a question: What kind of God does your doctrine of salvation reveal? He found it impossible to reconcile his doctrine of a God of love and grace with the view of a God limited by the logic of predestination. Charles was not willing to countenance any form of "limited redemption." Indeed, on July 12, 1741, he reported having declared "the *two great truths* of the everlasting gospel, universal redemption and Christian Perfection."[11] So we turn finally to this most critical aspect of Charles's doctrine of redemption.

Another hymn from his *Everlasting Love* collection (with Charles's own emphasis retained) reveals his pervasive emphasis on universal redemption for "all."

> Father, whose *everlasting love*
> Thy only Son for sinners gave,
> Whose grace *to all* did *freely* move,
> And sent him down a *world to save.*
>
> Help us thy mercy to extol,
> Immense, unfathomed, unconfined;
> To praise the Lamb who *died for all*,
> The *Savior of all humankind.*
>
> Thy *undistinguishing* regard
> Was cast on Adam's fallen race;
> *For all* thou hast in Christ prepared
> *Sufficient, sovereign, saving* grace.
>
> Jesus hath said, we *all* shall hope;
> Preventing grace for all is free;
> "And I, if I be lifted up,
> I will *draw all folk* unto me." (3)

John Wesley's sermon entitled *Free Grace*, arguably one of the best he ever wrote, aligned completely with Charles's view of God's

---

11. Kimbrough and Newport, *Manuscript Journal*, 1:319.

universal grace universally applied. To his sermon, published in 1739, John appended Charles's thirty-six-stanza hymn entitled "Universal Redemption." The central argument that runs through the lyrical text affirms that God's grace extends to all and that those who respond to that grace in faith will be saved. Charles articulates a third alternative, in other words, to a radical doctrine of election, on the one hand, in which only a few are saved, and a radical doctrine of universal salvation, on the other, in which everyone will be saved. Charles's proactive articulation of universal redemption pervades his hymns in pithy, forceful lines:

> For God hath bid all humankind
> His grace is for all
> My saving grace for all is free
> Pardon ye all in him may find
> For all my Lord was crucified
> For all, for all my Savior died!

No lines of Wesley's poetry annunciate this central theme more eloquently than these three stanzas of a hymn "After a Recovery":

> What shall I do my God to love,
>   My loving God to praise!
> The length, and breadth, and height to prove,
>   And depth of sovereign grace!
>
> Thy sovereign grace to all extends,
>   Immense and unconfined,
> From age to age it never ends,
>   It reaches all mankind.
>
> Throughout the world its breadth is known,
>   Wide as infinity,
> So wide, it never passed by one,
>   Or it had passed by me. (*HSP 1749*, 1:163)

God extends free, everlasting love to all. Christ died for all. God reaches out to everyone with sufficient, sovereign, saving grace. But how does one appropriate this grace? This question shapes the fundamental framework of Charles Wesley's way of salvation, and so we turn our attention in the next three chapters to the essential components of this dynamic relational and restorative process.

Questions for Consideration

1. What are the two central affirmations in Charles Wesley's hymn about the person and work of Christ?

2. What are the different theories of the atonement? How does Charles Wesley's approach reveal a multidimensional view or understanding of Christ's work?

3. On what biblical passages does Charles Wesley base his doctrine of the atonement? How are these passage subsequently woven into his hymns?

4. What does it mean to say that "humans love the wrong things in the wrong ways"? How does such an understanding express Wesley's doctrine of sin?

5. What are the images Wesley employs to describe the work of Christ on the cross?

6. How does Wesley's poetry utilize verbs to do the work and provide the power of his lyrical theology?

7. What is Charles Wesley's major disagreement with the Calvinists? What does this disagreement say about Wesley's view of God and the work of Christ pertaining to universal redemption? Share how his poem "On Recovery" speaks to this conviction.

three

Repentance: The Contrite Heart

THESE NEXT THREE CHAPTERS form a tight unit in Charles Wesley's lyrical theology. Having discussed two aspects of Charles's Christology—incarnation and redemption—we shift in these ensuing essays to the Wesleyan way of salvation—the appropriation of God's grace through repentance, justification, and sanctification.[1] Charles typically distinguishes between the "finished work of Christ"—the past, objective action—and the "unfinished work"—the present, subjective appropriation. He never conceived of atonement as the totality of Christ's redemptive work; rather, he viewed the cross and resurrection of Jesus Christ as the foundation

1. It is noteworthy that the scriptural allusions to these themes and the biblical texts from which Charles preached most frequently all have intimate connection to these three themes. The signature text for this chapter, Ezekiel 11:19, appears in his hymns more frequently than any other text. One could say it is his favorite hymn text. Mark 1:15, which deals with repentance, was his third favorite preaching text. The second most frequent biblical allusion in the hymns is Galatians 2:20–21 on the theme of sanctification. Charles's fourth and fifth favorite preaching texts, Matthew 11:28 and Luke 15:11, deal respectively with the themes of faith or justification and transformation or sanctification. In these chapters, therefore, we find ourselves in the center of Wesley's lyrical and discursive theology.

of God's present and transforming work through the Holy Spirit in the life of the believer. His eye was always firmly fixed on the goal of God's redemptive intervention. Charles, along with his brother, described this appropriation of God's redemptive grace as the way of salvation, of which repentance is the first component. So before we turn our attention directly to this third biblical theme, we must first review Charles's dynamic conception of this larger process of forgiveness and restoration.

From the "Finished" to the "Unfinished" Work of Christ

John Tyson has demonstrated how the finished work of Christ in Wesley's theology of redemption impinges on the interior life of those who seek salvation. "For Charles Wesley," he observes, "the atonement was not merely an historical truth to be believed, it was a transforming experience to be 'received' in the inner person."[2] Wesley viewed this movement from belief to reception as absolutely critical, because receiving God's grace and living into it fully was the ultimate goal. While he was concerned about how to properly interpret the "finished" work of Christ—his redemptive work that made atonement possible—he emphasized with equal or even greater urgency the "present" or "unfinished" work of Christ in the life of the believer. Despite the foundational nature of "Christ dying for us," he was equally concerned about "Christ reigning in us." "It was typical of Charles Wesley's dramatic approach to the theology of the cross," Tyson further observes, "that a shift from the past (Good Friday) to the present (the current experience) tense occurred in the same poem, verse, or even in the same line."[3] Wesley's doctrine of salvation, in other words, moves inevitably from the objective action of God-in-Christ toward the subjective appropriation of redemption; atonement leads to spiritual transformation.

2. Tyson, "'I Preached at the Cross,'" 207.
3. Ibid., 209.

The cross drove the sharp point of pathos deeper into the human heart than it had ever gone before. The ultimate confession of the early followers of Jesus was that somehow, mysteriously, God bore the sin and suffering of the world through the blood of the cross. Christ absorbed the agony of broken hearts and twisted lives for all time. For St. Paul, this was the revelation of God's *glory*, long hidden from everyone's eyes. As one well acquainted with suffering himself, he was determined only "to glory in the cross of Jesus Christ" (Gal 6:14), only "to proclaim Christ crucified" (1 Cor 1:23), to "know nothing" except this God who absorbs our wounds into his very being (1 Cor 2:2). In one of his many hymns on the cross Charles demonstrates how the historical act of Jesus finds ultimate expression in a profoundly personal confession of faith; his action establishes the most intimate of all relationships:

> O love divine, what hast thou done!
>   The immortal God hath died for me!
> The Father's co-eternal Son
>   Bore all my sins upon the tree;
> The immortal God for me hath died!
> My Lord, my love is crucified! (*HSP 1742*, 26)

All successive stanzas conclude with that impassioned profession of faith: "My Lord, my love is crucified!" Charles binds the way of salvation inextricably to the cross of Christ.

The Way of Salvation

The Wesleyan way of salvation, which Charles conceived of as a dynamic relational process, consists essentially in three dynamic movements—repentance, justification, and sanctification. The terms more typically used by both Charles and John with regard to these primary components of the way were repentance, faith, and holiness. Whichever terms are used, they define the Christian journey essentially, as we shall see, as homecoming. Despite the fact that everyone necessarily experiences the homeward pilgrimage in a different way, Charles believed that these three elements are essential to the journey.

Repentance

Those who possess a truly penitent spirit acknowledge their perennial posture *coram Deo* (before God). In this posture they experience the gaping chasm that separates the sinful creature from the Creator, yet find in God the One who is also close at hand and truly loves. Repentance carries a strong relational connotation, the initial turning of the heart and life homeward. Because God is a God who seeks to restore all things and is characterized by grace and love, as we have seen, the movement from repentance to faith is but a simple step.

Justification

Faith has to do with the capacity to entrust one's life fully to God. Charles often uses the word *faith* as a shorthand symbol for the more specific concept of justification by grace through faith. Drawing upon the teachings of his Anglican heritage Charles defined saving faith as a genuine "trust and confidence in the mercy of God through our Lord Jesus Christ and a steadfast hope of all good things at God's hand."[4] The center around which all else revolved for Wesley was the shared experience of faith-as-trust and salvation by grace.

Sanctification

Holiness is another shorthand term that refers to the whole process of becoming Christlike. Sanctification, therefore, implies a process of growing in grace and love. While justification by grace through faith is the foundation of the Christian life, sanctification is a process leading to holiness of heart and life. For Charles this

---

4. From the Homily of the Church of England titled "Of True Christian Faith," quoted in Outler, *John Wesley*, 130.

entails the fullest possible love of God and the fullest possible love of neighbor filling one's heart and life.

In this chapter, then, we will discover how Wesley conceived the first component of this journey of life in Christ—repentance—and we must begin with the reality and consequences of sin.

Depth of Mercy

In one of Charles's more familiar hymns, "Depth of Mercy," he plumbs the depths of the great mystery of God's mercy in response to the heart convicted of sin. He celebrates the nature of the One "whose property always is to have mercy." Wesley demonstrates his understanding of the struggle against sin. But his hymn also reflects his confidence in the God who picks up those whose spirits are broken and sustains them in their journey toward their true home.

> Depth of mercy! Can there be
> Mercy still reserved for me!
> Can my God his wrath forbear,
> Me, the chief of sinners spare!
>
> I my Master have denied,
> I afresh have crucified,
> Oft profaned his hallowed name,
> Put him to an open shame.
>
> There for me the Savior stands,
> Shows his wounds and spreads his hands,
> God is love! I know, I feel;
> Jesus weeps! But loves me still!
>
> Now incline me to repent,
> Let me now my fall lament,
> Now my foul revolt deplore,
> Weep, believe, and sin no more! (*HSP 1740*, 82–84)

In the context of his Anglican tradition, Charles had learned to pray, "We acknowledge and bewail our manifold sins and wickedness, which we from time to time most grievously have committed, by thought, word, and deed, against thy divine majesty, provoking most justly thy wrath and indignation against us. We do earnestly repent, and are heartily sorry for these our misdoings; the remembrance of them is grievous unto us, the burden of them is intolerable. Have mercy upon us, have mercy upon us, most merciful Father."[5] He believed that the heart of stone must be viewed within the larger reality of this depth of mercy.

The Heart of Stone

The biblical text alluded to by Wesley more often than any other in the *Collection* is Ezekiel 11:19: "And I will give them one heart, and I will put a new spirit within you; and I will take the stony heart out of their flesh, and will give them an heart of flesh." Nothing could demonstrate more clearly the Wesleyan focus on heart religion than this signature text. Many of the allusions to this text are found in two sections of the *Collection*. Hymns in these sections illustrate two themes, "Praying for Repentance" and "For Mourners Convinced of Sin." In the third stanza of the hymn "Sinners, obey the gospel-word," the singer prays for God to remove "the stony [heart]" (*HSP 1749*, 1:259). Wesley employs this particular image pervasively: "Break, this stony heart of mine"; "The stony from my heart remove"; "Take this heart of stone away." A positive supplication and affirmation accompanies this negative plea: "The grace be now on me bestowed, / The tender fleshly heart"; "'Tis thine a heart of flesh to give"; "Turn into flesh my heart of stone"; "Now the stone to flesh convert!" Something must convert the human heart turned to stone by sin. No greater impediment stands in the way of reconciliation with God.

Wesley maintains an extremely pessimistic view of the human condition. With Anselm, the great medieval archbishop of

5. This is the Prayer of Confession that Wesley prayed in every celebration of the sacrament of Holy Communion, from the *Book of Common Prayer*.

Canterbury, Charles laments, "You have not yet considered what a heavy weight sin is."[6] He draws his conclusion about the condition of humanity not only from his reading of scripture but also from his observation of life and human history. He defines sin in a traditional manner. Like his brother, John, he tended to emphasize the volitional aspect of sin—a willful transgression of a known law—and he asks God to defend him "from sin, from wilful sin alone." As Tyson states tersely, for Charles "sin was a problem of the human will; it involved an inward rebellion and a knowledgeable transgression."[7] He defined original sin in the single phrase "this rebel heart." He also frequently used the metaphor of illness or disease to communicate the serious nature of sin and also to prescribe its cure. In particular, the human disease of preoccupation with self can only be healed, he concluded, on the basis of some external force that both cures and reorients the child to the loving, parent God and away from self. The only force that can heal the human condition is love. Only love can break the heart of stone, calcified by the corrupting nature of sin.

The signature hymn on repentance reflects the centrality of the heart to the changes that only God can produce:

> O that I could repent,
> With all my idols part,
> And to thy gracious eye present
> An humble contrite heart!
> An heart with grief oppressed
> At having grieved my God,
> A troubled heart that cannot rest
> Till sprinkled with thy blood!
>
> Jesu, on me bestow
> The penitent desire,
> With true sincerity of woe,
> My aching breast inspire;

6. Anselm, *Cur Deus Homo*, 138.
7. Tyson, *Charles Wesley on Sanctification*, 52.

With softening pity look,
And melt my hardness down,
Strike with thy love's effectual stroke,
And break this heart of stone.

O for thy glorious name
My flinty bosom move,
And let me feel my load of shame,
And groan my want of love:
Low in the deepest deep
My humbled spirit lay,
And give me there to cry, and weep
My pensive life away. (*HSP 1749*, 1:143)

True religion is heart religion. Remorse, contrition, repentance—all happen primarily in the human heart. Those who focus on self harden their hearts towards God. The singer here prays for God to break the heart so that a truly penitent spirit can emerge out of the hard shell of self-deceit.

In this hymn Wesley echoes the Collect for Ash Wednesday in the Anglican *Book of Common Prayer*: "Create and make in us new and contrite hearts, that we, worthily lamenting our sins, and acknowledging our wretchedness, may obtain of thee, the God of all mercy, perfect remission and forgiveness." Another hymn from the same section of the *Collection* sounds this same note of penitence:

O that I could repent,
O that I could believe!
Thou, by thy voice, the marble rent,
The rock in sunder cleave!
Thou by thy two-edged sword
My soul and spirit part;
Strike, with the hammer of thy word,
And break my stubborn heart! (*HSP 1749*, 1:151)

In his explication of this hymn, Oliver Beckerlegge observed, "It is well to remember that in his journal for June 6, 1738, Charles Wesley said, 'I never knew the energy of sin till now that I experience the superior strength of Christ.' True repentance is the product, not the premise, of the Savior's entrance."[8] Here, as in other aspects of Wesley's theology, God's grace always precedes human experience or action. Repentance is actually a response to the grace of God already present. "Prevenient grace," that grace which comes before, graciously restores the capacity to choose the good. In these hymns, inward turning, as we shall see more fully, provides evidence for God's prevenient work in the soul. Wesley's lyrical reflection on Luke 3:8 enunciates this critical theme:

> Repentance is a grace
> Which flows from Christ alone,
> We cannot change the sinful race,
> Or mollify the stone:
> But if our God ordain,
> The rebels reconciled;
> Turned into flesh the hardened man,
> The stone into a child. (MS Luke, 42)

This view of the human condition and the solution to the problem resonate with the vision of the prophet Jeremiah, the goal of which was a heart for God: "I will put my law in their inward parts, and write it in their hearts" (31:33). Reflecting on this heart of flesh, Charles sings, "Thy Spirit's law of life divine, / O write it in my heart" (*Scripture Hymns*, 2:32). This kind of change requires a "turn."

Metanoia—Repentance as Turning

Another important passage from the prophecy of Ezekiel (18:31–32) also functioned as a source for Charles's concept of repentance: "Cast away from you all your transgressions, whereby ye have transgressed; and make you a new heart and a new spirit: for why

8. Hildebrandt and Beckerlegge, *Collection*, 207.

will ye die, O house of Israel? For I have no pleasure in the death of him that dieth, saith the Lord GOD: wherefore turn yourselves, and live ye." He framed no less than three hymns around this one text in the first section of the *Collection*, "Exhorting, and beseeching to return to God." In the hymns of this section Charles reinforces the constant refrain "Turn and live." No hymn develops this theme as fully as a lyrical paraphrase of Ezekiel's vision in Wesley's *Hymns on God's Everlasting Love* (1742). The fateful question is put to the child of God by each Person of the Trinity:

> Sinners turn, why will you die?
> God your Maker asks you why?
> God, who did your being give,
> Made you with himself to live;
> He the fatal cause demands,
> Asks the work of his own hands,
> Why, ye thankless creatures, why
> Will ye cross his love, and die?
>
> Sinners turn, why will you die?
> God your Savior asks you why?
> God, who did your souls retrieve,
> Died himself that you might live:
> Will you let him die in vain?
> Crucify your Lord again?
> Why, ye ransomed sinners, why
> Will ye slight his grace, and die?
>
> Sinners turn, why will you die?
> God the Spirit asks you why?
> God, who all your lives hath strove,
> Wooed you to embrace his love:
> Will you not the grace receive?
> Will you still refuse to live?
> Why, ye long-sought sinners, why
> Will ye grieve your God, and die? (43)

The Greek term used for repentance in the New Testament, *metanoia*, can also be translated "conversion." *Metonoia* connotes a force outside the self that turns it in another direction. In scripture, more often than not, repentance implies turning from the self to God and laying aside the old to put on the new. As S T Kimbrough observes concerning this hymn and this concept, "This hymn summarizes a lifelong plea of the Wesleys to the world in which they lived. It is the ancient cry of the prophets of Israel to God's people—*turn, turn, turn*! There is a need to change the direction one is going, namely, *away from God*, and to set one's course *toward God* and the divine will for one's own life and all creation."[9] Charles understood this turning to be closely related to one's self-understanding, and he found a poignant source for this idea in the biblical story of the prodigal son.

True Self-Understanding

Wesley found a clue to the deeper meaning of repentance—the stony heart, contrition, and the human need for true self-understanding. In a lyrical exposition on 1 John 1:8 he provides a window into the heart of every person:

> There is no truth in me.
> No true humility and love,
>   No true repentance I,
> No just or holy tempers prove,
>   But all I am is a lie. (MS Hymns NT, 120)

He realized, along with all others who understand any process of healing and restoration, that the first decisive step towards salvation is the acknowledgment of brokenness, the realization that sin is something for which all are deeply and inexcusably guilty. He came to the same conclusion as the Apostle John: "If we say that we have no sin, we deceive ourselves, and the truth is not in us" (1 John 1:8). The human proclivity to self-deception is great. But

9. Kimbrough, *Heart to Praise My God*, 167.

the denunciation of sin in general, particularly in others, only leads respectable people into self-righteousness. Charles also realized that threatening sinful people with damnation only creates fear and self-fixated concern. The wise and constructive note of Wesley's hymns and theology, as John Lawson has observed, revolved around his strategy "to speak of the greatness and majesty of the holy God, of his righteous claim that men and women should reverence, love, and serve him . . . and of the blessed offer of grace and hope."[10]

Both Charles's insight concerning the importance of true self-understanding and the loving appeal of his hymns to the human heart sprang from his interpretation of the parable of the prodigal son. Nowhere in scripture is the conviction of sin and repentance more poignantly expressed than in this familiar narrative in Luke 15. The prodigal, stripped of dignity, value, and identity, at long last "came to himself" (15:17)—and this is the critical turning point in his life, and in the story. In the depth of his despair he remembered who he was and to whom he belonged, but that rediscovery was a two-edged sword. On the one hand, he realized how far he had strayed and was overcome with a sense of guilt and shame; on the other hand, his true self-understanding revealed the fact that nothing could ever strip him of his primary and eternal identity as his father's son. His act of penitence marked the reclamation of his true identity.

True self-understanding came to the prodigal in an instant as a consequence of God's grace. In a lyrical paraphrase of this story in Wesley's *Scripture Hymns*, the poet reveals the depth of this discovery:

> Yes, from this instant now I will
> To my offended Father cry:
> My base ingratitude I feel,
> Vilest of all thy children I,
> Not worthy to be called thy son,
> Yet will I thee my Father own.

10. Lawson, *Wesley Hymns*, 98–99.

If thou hast willed me to return,
　　If weeping at thy feet I fall,
The prodigal in justice spurn,
　　Or pity and forgive me all,
In answer to my friend above,
In honor of his bleeding love. (2:6)

That moment of self-awareness in the pigsty disclosed the seductive villainy of sin. Charles unmasks the reality of evil temptations: "Their joy is all sadness, their mirth is all vain / Their laughter is madness, their pleasure is pain!" (*Redemption Hymns*, 32). This discovery pales in significance, however, to the discovery of the merciful, forgiving, and loving character of God in the story. "Ready the Father is to own," Charles exclaims, "and kiss his late-returning son" (*HSP 1749*, 1:259)!

Charles celebrates these discoveries in a "Hymn of Thanksgiving to the Father":

Father, behold thy son,
　　In Christ I am thy own.
Stranger long to thee and rest,
　　See the prodigal is come:
Open wide thine arms and breast,
　　Take the weary wanderer home.

Thine eye observed from far,
　　Thy pity looked me near:
Me thy mercies yearned to see,
　　Me thy mercy ran to find,
Empty, poor, and void of thee,
　　Hungry, sick, and faint, and blind.

Thou on my neck didst fall,
　　Thy kiss forgave me all:
Still the gracious words I hear,

Words that made the Savior mine,
"Haste, for him the robe prepare,
His be righteousness divine"! (*HSP 1739*, 107–8)

Conviction of sin leads to pardon. In the same way that those who come to themselves experience true self-understanding in a moment, those who are justified by grace through faith experience God's pardon in a moment as well. The grace that facilitates repentance, that first step in the way that leads home, also facilitates the experience of God's unconditional love. As we move next to a discussion of justification, the second dimension of the way of salvation, we sing, "And turn with zealous haste, and run / Into the outstretched arms of God" (*HSP 1742*, 299).

Questions for Consideration

1. How does Charles Wesley distinguish between the "finished work of Christ" and the "unfinished work" of Christ, or between past, objective action and present, subjective appropriation?

2. What is Charles Wesley's view of salvation? How do both John and Charles articulate this dynamic relational process in terms of repentance, justification, and sanctification? How does such a view express the distinctive doctrines of Methodism?

3. How does Charles Wesley understand faith and the relationship of faith to the life of holiness or sanctification?

4. How does Charles Wesley's hymn "Depth of Mercy" demonstrate both the depths of divine love and the struggle against sin?

5. What signature biblical text conveys Wesley's focus on heart religion?

6. What is prevenient grace? What is the role of prevenient grace in restoring the soul to God? How are repentance and prevenient grace related?

7. What other key biblical passages does Wesley utilize to communicate the divine-human relationship and the themes of repentance and change?

8. How does Charles Wesley's use of the parable of the prodigal son communicate his understanding of grace and sin and his identity as a child of God?

four

Justification: God's Grace and Living Faith

CHARLES WESLEY LOCATES JUSTIFICATION—THE second component in the way of salvation—within the larger sphere of God's faithfulness and what the writer of the Letter to the Hebrews describes as "the new and living way." Hebrews 10:19–22, a part of the preface to the biblical author's larger discussion of faith in chapters 11 and 12, functions as Charles's signature text for this theme.

> Therefore, my friends, since we have confidence to enter the sanctuary by the blood of Jesus, by the new and living way that he opened for us through the curtain (that is, through his flesh), and since we have a great priest over the house of God, let us approach with a true heart in full assurance of faith, with our hearts sprinkled clean from an evil conscience and our bodies washed with pure water.

This passage ranks seventh among those most alluded to in the *Collection*. In quite a number of his poetic compositions he describes faith, along the lines of Hebrews, as "the gift unspeakable."

In a hymn entitled "The Life of Faith," Wesley's signature hymn for this theme, he describes the origins and nature of faith. Faith is a source of knowledge concerning God and the way in which God offers salvation, hope, and healing to humanity. It illuminates the child of God and enables spiritual vision. Wesley affirms that faith is a gift, something related to the burning presence of the Spirit in the lives of the faithful.

> Author of faith, eternal Word,
>> Whose Spirit breathes the active flame,
> Faith, like its Finisher and Lord,
>> Today as yesterday the same.
>
> To thee our humble hearts aspire,
>> And ask the gift unspeakable;
> Increase in us the kindled fire,
>> In us the work of faith fulfill. (*HSP 1740*, 6)

Faith is a complex reality in the lives of people, but it is also quite simple. Like so many other great Christian teachers, Wesley links the gift of faith with the capacity to trust God.

He also uses the term *faith* as a shorthand expression for the concept of justification by grace through faith.[1] He viewed justification by faith as the door through which the believer passes into a vital relationship with God through Christ. Trust in Christ, he firmly believed, establishes a right relationship with God and instills confidence in believers, enabling them to sing, "No condemnation now I dread; / Jesus, and all in him, is mine" (*HSP 1739*, 118). It provides "a true heart in full assurance of faith," freedom from a burdened conscience, and spiritual cleansing, to allude to the Hebrews text. When people put their faith in Christ—when they accept God's unconditional love offered freely to them in Christ—a proper love of God, others, and themselves begins to "warm their heart."

In the same way that the author of the Letter to the Hebrews defines faith as "the assurance of things hoped for, the conviction

---

1. See Chilcote, "Wesley and the Language of Faith," 299–319.

of things not seen" (11:1), Wesley understood living faith to be a sure *trust* and *confidence* in the mercy and steadfast love of God, a theme explored in the remaining stanzas of the hymn.

> By faith we know thee strong to save,
>> (Save us, a present Savior thou!)
> Whate'er we hope, by faith we have,
>> Future and past subsisting now.

> To all that in thy name believe,
>> Eternal life with thee is given,
> Into themselves they all receive,
>> Pardon, and happiness, and heaven.

> The things unknown to feeble sense,
>> Unseen by reason's glimmering ray,
> With strong, commanding evidence
>> Their heavenly origin display.

> Faith lends its realizing light,
>> The clouds disperse, the shadows fly,
> The invisible appears in sight,
>> And God is seen by mortal eye. (6–7)

Four particular themes characterize Wesley's understanding of faith and demonstrate the essential Anglican orientation of his lyrical theology and doctrinal language: the priority of grace, the concept of true and lively faith, the doctrine of justification by faith, and the vision of faith working by love.

The Priority of Grace

As one may well expect, many of Wesley's *Redemption Hymns* in particular focus on the central issue of faith and how the gift of faith restores fellowship with God. In "Father of Jesus Christ the just" he demonstrates how faith "works" and how God brings about new creation through this gracious gift. Since salvation has to do with God's act and the human response, he shows how divine grace and human faith relate to one another in the process of salvation. In this hymn he celebrates two theological convictions. First, the priority of grace—God's grace flows to all people; God excludes no one from this offer of relationship. Second, the personal or autobiographical nature of faith—authentic faith must be "mine." Because Jesus died for *all*, he died for *me*!

> Father of Jesus Christ the just,
>> My friend and Advocate with thee,
> Pity a soul who fain would trust
>> In him, who loved, and died for me;
> But only you can make him known,
> And in my heart reveal your Son. (18)

Wesley begins the drama of redemption with God and not with the human being. Jesus, our friend and advocate, first loved and "died for me." Despite the fact that Christ has earned our trust, entrusting our lives to him is hard. Grace initiates the process of redemption, God reaching out to us even before we are capable of response, as we have already seen.

> If drawn by your alluring grace,
>> My want of living faith I feel,
> Show me in Christ your smiling face;
>> What flesh and blood can ne'er reveal,
> Your co-eternal Son display,
> And call my darkness into day. (18)

God envelops everyone in grace; grace is God's wooing activity. It convicts sinners of their lack of faith, reveals the "smiling face" of Jesus, and calls them out of the darkness into God's marvelous light.

> The gift unspeakable impart,
>> Command the light of faith to shine,
> To shine in my dark drooping heart,
>> And fill me with the life divine;

> Now bid the new creation be,
> O God, let there be faith in me! (19)

In creation God sings, "Let there be light." In redemption or re-creation God commands "the light of faith to shine." The concluding couplet emphasizes the inseparable nature of God's grace in creation and redemption. It also celebrates the cosmic nature of redemption in Christ.

Wesley coined a turn of phrase in the following stanza that provides an amazing insight: "You without faith I cannot please; / Faith without you I cannot have" (19). Faith entails paradox. Those who fail to put their trust in God remain alienated, unhappy, and insecure in life. But the wonder of God's plan of redemption is that God supplies all we need but cannot provide for ourselves. D. M. Baillie called this the "paradox of grace."[2] Without God, faith could never be awakened in the soul. But the gift of faith that God freely offers restores fellowship with God.

> But you have sent the Prince of Peace
> To seek my wandering soul, and save;
> O Father! Glorify your Son,
> And save me for his sake alone! (19)

True and Lively Faith

Wesley distinguished between "dead" and "living" faith. Faith is not simply what we say we believe; it is the dynamic foundation of our relationship with God. Whether described as the "experience of faith," "faith of the gospel," "spirit of faith," or simply "faith"—various expressions found throughout Wesley's writings—all connote the experience of having been accepted and pardoned by God through faith in Christ alone. The foundation of this concept is trust (*fiducia*). Faith is the gift of trust—the Spirit enabling the alienated children of God to entrust their lives to God's loving care. Many people think that faith refers simply to a set of beliefs

2. Baillie, *God Was in Christ*, 114–18.

to which Christians subscribe. While the term *faith* can be used in this sense as assent to certain propositions, Charles emphasized faith as the foundation of a life-giving relationship that has power and energy. To put faith in Christ means, quite simply, to rely on him completely, to put one's whole trust in him. Those who entrust their lives to Christ in this way experience forgiveness, feel reconciled to God, and know that all of life remains secure in him because of his great love for every person.

Wesley makes a second, significant distinction as well. Nowhere in his writings or sacred poems does he distinguish explicitly between faith and belief, but the distinction is implied throughout. He differentiates between the "faith in which one believes" (*fides quae creditur*) and the "faith by which one believes" (*fides qua creditur*). The contrast here is not so much between a dead and a living faith as it is between an objective faith (what might be described as *the* faith, or a system of belief) and a subjective faith (what Wesley describes as a living or saving faith). As important as it is to believe in certain things (the so-called substance of faith), Wesley pointed to the act of faith, or that living faith by which one believes, as the foundation of the Christian life. While faith and belief are integral—never to be separated from one another—Charles always gives priority to the "enpersonalization" of faith—making faith one's own. *The* faith must become, at some point and in a dynamic way, *my* faith.

Justification by Faith

Wesley's concept of justification by faith itself revolves around Romans 3:23–24: "Since all have sinned and fall short of the glory of God; they are now justified by his grace as a gift, through the redemption that is in Christ Jesus." His discoveries with regard to justification by grace through faith were profoundly autobiographical. His sermon on this Romans text provides one of his most vigorous discussions of his doctrine of justification. After having described the corrupt and fallen condition of the human creature, Wesley describes justification by faith as the remedy for this sickness and tersely summarizes his position by quoting the Anglican Article of Religion XI, "Of the Justification of Man": "We are accounted righteous before God, only for the merit of our Lord Jesus Christ through faith, and not for our own works or deservings. Wherefore, that we are justified by faith only, is a most wholesome doctrine, and very full of comfort."[3]

Charles discovered all of this, like his brother John, in 1738. On the threshold of his transformative spiritual awakening of May 21 he was pondering the doctrinal statements about justification in the most critical Anglican documents, like the Article, on the subject. He had already accepted this doctrine as true when God transformed his intellectual assent into a vital experience by virtue of which he could claim, "I saw that by faith I stood; by the continual support of faith, which kept me from falling, though of myself I am ever sinking into sin."[4] One can often hear autobiographical echoes in the hymns:

> I hold thee with a trembling hand,
>> But will not let thee go
> Till steadfastly by faith I stand,
>> And all thy goodness know. (*HSP 1740*, 156)

"By faith I every moment stand," Charles sings, "strangely upheld by thy right hand" (*HSP 1742*, 171).

Originally written to help distinguish the Wesleyan way from that of the Moravians, one of Wesley's "Hymns for One Convinced of Unbelief" celebrates this theme:

> Author of faith, to thee I cry,
> To thee, who wouldst not have me die,
>> But know the truth and live;
> Open mine eyes to see thy face,
> Work in my heart the saving grace,
>> The life eternal give.
>
> I know the work is only thine—

3. "Sermon 6: Romans 3:23–24," in Newport, *Sermons*, 199.
4. Kimbrough and Newport, *Manuscript Journal,* 1:102.

> The gift of faith is all divine;
>> But if on thee we call
>> Thou wouldst the benefit bestow,
>> And give us hearts to feel and know
>>> That thou hast died for all.
>
> Be it according to thy word!
> Now let me find my pardoning Lord,
>> Let what I ask be given;
>> The bar of unbelief remove,
>> Open the door of faith and love,
>>> And take me into heaven! (*HSP 1749*, 1:42–43)

On its most rudimentary level justification by grace through faith entails pardon, liberation, and the assurance of God's love.

Justification as Pardon—the Door of Faith

In his discussion of justification in Charles Wesley's doctrine of redemption, John Tyson makes a very interesting observation with regard to Charles's use of the image of pardon in his hymns.[5] Despite the fact that the term *pardon* is not even found in the New Testament and seldom used in the Old, it is one of Wesley's favorite terms related to justification. *Pardon* is a legal term, synonymous with forgiveness, acquittal, and justification, and is related to the concepts of mercy, reconciliation, ransom, and redemption.

> His love we proclaim, and publish abroad,
> The blood of the Lamb hath brought us to God:
> He purchased our pardon, who died in our stead,
> The uttermost farthing our surety hath paid. (*HSP 1749*, 2:180)

God graciously forgives those who have no claim to pardon and can hardly expect it.

Paul Tillich, a great twentieth-century theologian, once said that the most difficult thing in life is to accept the fact that we are

---

5. See Tyson, *Charles Wesley on Sanctification*, 98–102.

accepted. Wesley acknowledges how difficult this is for mc
ple. He interfaces the reality of forgiveness offered with the
ence of pardon accepted, reflecting on the pathos of the stat......ent
"Lord, I believe; help thou my unbelief" (Mark 9:24).

> Lord, I believe, thou *wilt* forgive,
>> But help me to believe thou *dost*:
> The answer of thy promise give,
>> Wherein thou causest me to trust,
> The gospel-faith divine impart,
>> Which seals my pardon on my heart. (*Scripture Hymns*, 2:205)

Through a gracious act of mercy God does for sinners what they cannot do for themselves. Those who trust in Christ experience forgiveness as pardon. Our acceptance of the fact that God has already accepted us and loves us is the essence of the act of faith.

Christ came, therefore, to demonstrate the depth of God's mercy and love. Charles articulates the essence of forgiveness and pardon in this lyrical paraphrase of Revelation 22:17—the Spirit's gift of the water of life:

> As soon as in him we believe,
>> By faith of his Spirit we take,
> And freely forgiven, receive
>> The mercy for Jesus's sake;
> We gain a pure drop of his love,
>> The life of eternity know,
> Angelical happiness prove,
>> And witness an heaven below. (*Scripture Hymns*, 2:431)

Justification, and the concomitant experience of pardon, functions like a door that opens for the forgiven into a new world of grace and peace. The immediate biblical allusion upon which Charles draws is the apostles' report of their evangelistic labors upon return to Antioch and their celebration of the way in which God "opened a door of faith for the Gentiles" (Acts 14:27).

He hath opened a door

To the penitent poor,

And rescued from sin,

And admitted the harlots and publicans in:

They have heard the glad sound,

They have liberty found

Through the blood of the Lamb,

And plentiful pardon in Jesus's name.
(*Redemption Hymns*, 4)

One stanza concludes with a typical statement from Charles's pen: "And embrace the glad tidings of pardon and peace!" (4).

Justification as Liberation—the Power of Faith

Wesley's hymn originally titled "Free Grace" is one of the most significant lyrical expositions of justification in the history of Christian song. It treats this theme in a magisterial way and identifies liberation as one of the most important experiences related to redemption in Christ.

And can it be, that I should gain

An interest in the Savior's blood!

Died he for me, who caused his pain?

For me? Who him to death pursued?

Amazing love! How can it be

That thou, my God, shouldst die for me? (*HSP 1739*, 117)

This emphatic question about our "share" in redemption shapes the whole of Wesley's theology. The questions that follow amplify the extraordinary nature and the full extent of God's love for the sinner. The fourth stanza of the hymn celebrates the liberation that Christ offers to all. The allusions to the story of Paul and Silas in Acts 16 are unmistakable:

Long my imprisoned spirit lay,

Fast bound in sin and nature's night;

> Thine eye diffused a quickening ray;
>   I woke, the dungeon flamed with light;
> My chains fell off, my heart was free,
> I rose, went forth, and followed thee. (118)

In a lyrical paraphrase of Psalm 88:8 Wesley echoes the language of "Free Grace":

> My soul shall quit this dark abode
>   The moment I believe;
> The chains of sin fall off my heart,
>   And freed by love divine,
> My only Lord and God thou art,
>   And I am wholly thine. (MS Hymns OT, 62)

The believer experiences God's work of grace in justification, therefore, not only as forgiveness and pardon but also as liberation. In many of his hymns Charles exploits a familiar biblical event to describe the liberating experience of grace: the deliverance of the Israelites from bondage in Egypt. In a lyrical allegory of the exodus the sinner implores God thus: "Drown all my sins in the Red Sea, / And bring me safe to land" (*HSP* 1749, 1:44). Wesley employs the language of emancipation with uncommon power. The power of faith is a power that liberates, and the manumission imagery not only describes deliverance from the bondage of sin, it identifies gratitude and assurance as parallel gifts of God's love in Christ.

Justification and Assurance—the Solace of Faith

The italicized words in the following stanza reflect two critical concerns for Wesley related to the impact of justifying faith in the life of the believer. They can be formulated in one pressing question: How can I *know* that God loves *me*? The issues of assurance and personalization figured prominently in Charles's effort to communicate the redeeming love of God.

> How can we sinners *know*
> Our sins on earth forgiven?

How can my gracious Savior show
   My name inscribed in heaven?
   What we have felt and seen,
   With confidence we tell,
And publish to the ends of earth
   The signs infallible.

   We who in Christ believe
   That he for us hath died,
We all his unknown peace receive
   And feel his blood applied.

. . . .

   We by his Spirit prove
   And know the things of God,
The things which freely of his love
   He hath on us bestowed. (*HSP* 1749, 2:220)

This stunning hymn on "the marks of faith" correlates knowing and feeling. Both of these words are critical to Charles with regard to the experience and understanding of sin and forgiveness—of justification. Almost from the beginning, the issue of assurance had been central to his pursuit of God. Assurance figured very prominently in his religious experience of May 1738, just as it had for his brother. This internal dynamic of assurance—to know we are secure in God's love—dominates the landscape of redemption for both Wesleys. The internal sense of peace and assurance that normally accompanies the experience of justification may be described as the solace of faith.

Charles was always strongly predisposed in the direction of what he and John both called "inward religion."[6] His biblical reference point for this interiority was 1 John 2:3: "Hereby we do know that we know him." For Charles, authentic life with God meant to be known and to know, and this inferred assurance. He believed

6. See the editors' illuminating note on this topic in Hildebrandt and Beckerlegge, *Collection*, 196.

that the soul craves for a faith that enables one to cry out, "I know whom I have believed" (2 Tim 1:12). Moreover, his wise grasp of the ways of God led him to the conclusion that justification by grace through faith—with its attendant assurance—leads to fuller obedience to the law of God and not release from this obligation. The full verse from 1 John quoted above concludes: "we do know that we know him, if we obey his commandments." Believers who are able to cry out, "Abba, Father" make their faith effective by loving as Jesus loves.

Faith Working by Love

> Stand we in the good old way,
>   Who Christ by faith receive,
> Heartily we must obey,
>   If truly we believe:
> Other way can none declare
> Than this from which we ne'er will move:
>   Saved by grace through faith we are,
>   Through faith that works by love. (*Scripture Hymns*, 2:13)

In this hymn based on Jeremiah 6:16 Charles articulates one of the most central themes in Wesleyan theology—faith working by love, a concept drawn from Galatians 5:6. The effort to hold "faith alone" and "holy living" together was a delicate balancing act. This concern was the principle theme of Wesley's sermon on Titus 3:8. In his exposition of this text, among the marks or effects of true faith, he includes inward peace of conscience; joy; liberty, not only from the guilt but also from the power of sin; and love, for "faith works by love, and he that loveth not knoweth not God, for God is love." He concludes his sermon with these poignant words:

> Show your faith by your good works. Without these all pretensions to faith are false. These are the necessary effects or fruits or signs of a living faith. Necessary they are, not to justify us before God, but to justify us before others; or rather, not to make, but to show us acceptable;

not as the cause but as the evidence of our new birth; not as conditions, but consequences and tokens of our salvation. The faith that does not work by love is an idle, barren, dead faith. It is no faith at all.[7]

Faith, in other words, is a means to love's end. Charles's poetic reflections on Ephesians 2:8–10 provide the most memorable lyrical expression of this central theme. His "Love-Feast" hymn describes faith as an ongoing, life-transforming experience, something for which the child of God yearns and stretches forward to receive as a gift.

> Plead we thus for faith alone,
> Faith which by our works is shown;
> God it is who justifies,
> Only faith the grace applies,
>
> Active faith that lives within,
> Conquers hell, and death, and sin,
> Hallows whom it first made whole,
> Forms the Savior in the soul.
>
> Let us for this faith contend,
> Sure salvation, is its end;
> Heaven already is begun,
> Everlasting life is won:
>
> Only let us persevere
> Till we see our Lord appear,
> Never from the Rock remove,
> Saved by faith which works by love. (HSP 1740, 184)

7. "Sermon 5: Titus 3:8," in Newport, Sermons, 150–51.

Questions for Consideration

1. How is Charles Wesley's view of justification grounded in his use of Hebrews 10:19–22? How does Wesley's hymn "The Life of Faith" communicate this view as well?

2. How does Charles Wesley understand the life of faith?

3. What are two aspects of Wesley's conviction about the priority of grace?

4. What is the relationship between Wesley's view of prevenient grace and the role of justifying grace in the process of redemption?

5. What does Charles Wesley consider "true and lively faith"?

6. How does Charles Wesley's hymn on "unbelief" express the "conjunctive nature" of the life of faith as both divine gift and human response?

7. How does the image of the porch, the door, and the house communicate the key Methodist doctrines of repentance, justification, and holiness?

8. How is Wesley's doctrine of assurance related to the ways in which the believer comes to know God? What in the hymn "The Marks of Faith" provides such insight? How is such knowledge of God possible?

9. One of the key themes in Wesleyan theology is "faith working through love": how does Wesley hold faith and love together as a dynamic expression of the life of holiness?

five

Sanctification: The Process of Renewal

CHARLES WESLEY, LIKE MANY Anglican theologians, looks at all aspects of Christian faith from a both/and perspective. In his concept of the way of salvation Charles attempts to hold together aspects of the Christian faith that are easily and often torn apart. He links the biblical concept of justification, which we have just explored, with its necessary counterpart—sanctification in the life of the believer. The term *sanctification* simply means "to be made holy." In Wesley's lyrical theology it refers to that process by which the faithful Christian becomes more and more like Jesus through the shaping influence of the Holy Spirit.

In two stanzas of his twenty-eight-stanza hymn "The Promise of Sanctification," the signature hymn for this theme, Charles describes this essential heart work of the Spirit as a process of renewal:

> Thy sanctifying Spirit pour
> To quench my thirst, and wash me clean;
> Now, Father, let the gracious shower
> Descend, and make me pure from sin.

Give me a new, a perfect heart,

From doubt, and fear, and sorrow free,

The mind which was in Christ impart,

And let my spirit cleave to thee.

("Promise of Sanctification," 45)

Randy Maddox reflects on the significance of this hymn: "One of the characteristic emphases of both John and Charles Wesley was that God offers all who seek it not only assurance of the forgiveness of their sins but also transformation of their dispositions and desires, enabling them to take on the 'mind of Christ' and the 'fruit of the Spirit.' In technical terms, the gift of salvation includes not only justification, or imputed holiness, but also sanctification, or imparted holiness."[1] Wesley's way of salvation, therefore, entails both forgiveness and restoration. Not only is it forensic (dealing with the moral chasm that separates broken humanity from God), it is also therapeutic (dealing with the diseased nature of the human being, restoring original health and wholeness). Without justification/forgiveness God's relationship with the fallen child cannot be put right; without sanctification/holiness God's original design for humanity cannot be realized. Faith in Christ establishes a new relationship between God and the faithful disciple, but God calls those who have been forgiven into the deepest possible love of God and others. Sanctification is the process; holiness of heart and life, or Christian perfection, is the goal.

In this chapter on sanctification we will review this process and in the final chapter of this study we will explore perfection, the ultimate goal toward which this process moves. The healing process of sanctification—the one thing needful—begins with new birth, is sustained by the indwelling Spirit, and entails growth in grace and love.

1. Maddox, editorial introduction to Wesley, "Promise of Sanctification."

The One Thing Needful

Charles preached on the narrative of Jesus's encounter with Mary and Martha recorded in the tenth chapter of St. Luke's Gospel more than any other story in the New Testament. He shared a sermon on "The One Thing Needful" with his brother John based on Luke 10:42.[2] The central point of this sermon is that the "renewal of our fallen nature" or "the restoration of the image of God" is the one thing needful. "To recover our first estate, from which we are thus fallen, is the one thing now needful—to re-exchange the image of Satan for the image of God, bondage for freedom, sickness for health. . . . The one work we have to do is to return from the gates of death to perfect soundness; to have our diseases cured, our wounds healed, and our uncleanness done away."[3] "This sermon also hints," claims Barrie Tabraham, "at the way in which Charles would develop his ideas on sanctification and Christian perfection."[4] Wesley based this elevation of renewal and restoration on three critical facts that he discerned in the biblical witness: (1) God created human beings for the purpose of love; (2) Christ died, rose, and ascended to heal and liberate, to secure human happiness and immortality; and (3) the Spirit works through the dispensations of providence to restore health, liberty, and holiness in all people.

In 2 Corinthians 3:17–18, Wesley's signature text for the theme of sanctification, St. Paul describes this one thing needful as a process of restoration: "Now the Lord is the Spirit, and where the Spirit of the Lord is, there is freedom. And all of us, with unveiled faces, seeing the glory of the Lord as though reflected in a mirror, are being transformed into the same image from one degree of glory to another; for this comes from the Lord, the Spirit." In a lyrical paraphrase of this text Charles pleads,

> Come then, and dwell in me,
> Spirit of power within,

---

2. See Chilcote, "'All the Image of Thy Love,'" 21–40.

3. "Sermon 21: Luke 10:42," in Newport, *Sermons*, 364.

4. Tabraham, *Brother Charles*, 58.

And bring the glorious liberty
From sorrow, fear, and sin:
The seed of sin's disease,
Spirit of health, remove,
Spirit of finished holiness,
Spirit of perfect love. (*Scripture Hymns*, 2:298)

New Birth

In the development of his own views about this necessary regeneration Charles closely follows the understanding of this doctrine outlined in John's sermon on "the new birth." He summarizes the conjunction discussed above in two simple points. First, God forgives through Christ. Second, God renews through the Spirit. Both of these movements of salvation are important. In fact, Charles believed that an emphasis on the former without equal attention given to the latter jeopardizes God's original design for humanity. The gift of new birth must accompany the "former gift" of faith; otherwise, restoration cannot be properly effected:

Thy former gift is vain,
Unless thou lift me up,
Begetting me again
Unto a lively hope;
O let me know that second birth,
And live the life of heaven on earth.

I wait thy will to do
As angels do in heaven,
In Christ a creature new,
Eternally forgiven;
I wait thy perfect will to prove,
When sanctified by sinless love. (*HSP 1749*, 1:211–12)

Forgiveness and restoration must be held together; not attending to this dynamic balance truncates the gospel.

In the Wesleyan way of salvation justification by faith and regeneration, or new birth, are effected simultaneously. Despite the fact that these two aspects of the salvific process are inseparable, it is important to distinguish the "two sides of the one coin." The experience of justification reflects a relative change; it changes the believer's relationship with God. New birth entails a real change. Having entrusted their lives to Christ, believers begin to experience change from the inside out. They begin a process of becoming more and more like Jesus. Charles attributes this work of grace to the Trinity:

> See a sinful worm of earth!
>   Bless her for the laving flood,
> Plunge her by a second birth
>   Into the depths of God.

> Let the promised inward grace
>   Accompany the sign,
> On her new-born soul impress
>   The glorious name divine:
> Father, all thy love reveal,
>   Jesus all thy mind impart,
> Holy Ghost, renew, and dwell
>   Forever in her heart. (HSP 1749, 2:246)

The Father reveals the love; the Son imparts his mind; the Spirit renews and indwells the faithful.

Despite this important theological point—that all three Persons of the Trinity are involved in this process—Wesley tends to identify the work of restoration, as in the hymn above, with the Holy Spirit, a somewhat natural connection to which scripture attests as well. In a hymn for those "groaning for the spirit of adoption" he describes the Holy Spirit's role:

> O that the Comforter would come,

> Nor visit as a transient guest,
> But fix in me his constant home,
> And take possession of my breast,
> And make my soul his loved abode,
> The temple of indwelling God.
>
> Come, Holy Ghost, my heart inspire,
> Attest that I am born again!
> Come, and baptize me now with fire,
> Or all your former gifts are vain.
> I cannot rest in sin forgiven;
> Where is the earnest of *my* heaven! (*HSP 1740*, 132)

In Wesley's view the Holy Spirit functions like the midwife of the new birth. This spiritual regeneration parallels the process of physical birth. A long process precedes it, and growth and development follow thereafter.

"New" or "second" birth is the first step in the process of sanctification. This concept even appears in Charles's most famous Christmas hymn, "Hark! the herald angels sing."

> Mild he lays his glory by,
> Born that we no more may die,
> Born to raise us from the earth,
> Born to give us second birth. (*HSP 1739*, 207)

The poetic and biblical image of second birth connotes a range of ideas. It symbolizes the fragility of the "infant Christian." "Hangs my new-born soul on thee," Charles observes, "Weak as helpless infancy" (*Scripture Hymns*, 1:264). In a lyrical reflection on James 2:25 the image serves to demonstrate the presence and power of God's grace in human weakness:

> While thus the life of faith she showed
> Throughout her new-born soul displayed,
> She felt that hallowing grace of God,
> By which our faith is perfect made,

By which we truly righteous prove,
And then salute the saints above. (*Scripture Hymns*, 2:385)

Charles's lyrical rendering of "Thy will be done in earth, as it is in heaven" (Matt 6:10) signals a change of the will as a consequence of grace bestowed:

The graces of my second birth
To me shall all be given,
And I shall do thy will on earth,
As angels do in heaven. (*HSP 1742*, 232)

Perhaps most importantly, the new birth represents the promise of seeds sown by the activity of the Spirit and the hope of fruit to come:

Jesu, fulfill the gospel-word,
In us thou beauteous branch arise,
Arise, thou planting of the Lord,
Be glorious in thy people's eyes.

O root divine, in this our earth
Spring up, and yield a fair increase,
The graces of our second birth,
The goodly fruits of righteousness. (*HSP 1742*, 187)

God the Spirit is the instrument of transformation and the presence of the Spirit facilitates continuous growth toward deeper levels of love.

The Indwelling Spirit

Wesley frequently quotes St. Paul's declaration in Galatians 2:20, "Yet not I, but Christ liveth in me." The Spirit sanctifies believers by indwelling their lives. The glorious liberty that accompanies the Spirit not only frees from sorrow, fear, and sin, but also liberates believers to love fully. In the process of sanctification there is, to use the language of classical spiritual formation, an apophatic (emptying) and kataphatic (filling) rhythm. God empties the faithful of the old and fills them with the new.

> Lord, we believe; and wait the hour
>> That brings the promised grace,
> When born of God we sin no more,
>> But always see thy face.
>
> Since thou wouldst have us free from sin,
>> And pure as those above,
> Make haste to bring thy nature in,
>> And perfect us in love. (*HSP 1749*, 2:189)

The Spirit consumes, blots out, erases, and drives out sins, emptying the follower of Christ of all that separates him or her from God. A collection of "Hymns for Those that Wait for Full Redemption" supplies quite a number of hymns that illustrate this effect of the indwelling Spirit. The closing stanzas of the second hymn in this section express the confidence of the believer in God's ability to perform this spiritual surgery.

> Bounds I will not set to thee,
>> Shorten thine almighty hand:
> Save from all iniquity,
>> Let not sin's foundations stand,
> Every stone o'erturn, o'erthrow;
> I believe it *may* be so.
>
> Wilt thou lop the boughs of sin,
>> Leaving still the stock behind?
> No, thy love shall work within,
>> Quite expel the carnal mind,
> Root and branch destroy my foe;
> I believe it *shall* be so. (*HSP 1749*, 2:149)

In Wesleyan theology, however, God empties for the purpose of filling. The indwelling Spirit fills the follower of Christ with the

Lord's mind and righteousness, restores the image of Christ, and teaches the disciple how to love.[5] "Into sin I cannot fall," observes Wesley, "while hanging on thy love" (*Scripture Hymns*, 2:410). In a sacred poem on the indwelling Spirit he asks God to "form thy Son in me, / And perfect me in love" (*HSP 1742*, 254). He underscores the kataphatic nature of the process of sanctification in one of his hymns on full redemption:

> Lord, we believe, and rest secure,
>   Thine utmost promises to prove,
> To rise restored, and throughly pure,
>   In all the image of thy love,
> Filled with the glorious life unknown,
> Forever sanctified in one. (*HSP 1749*, 2:187)

Charles embraces the scriptural promise for God to deliver the faithful fully from sin and to fill them completely with the love of Christ.

Growth in Grace and Love

Sanctification, in Wesley's view, is a lengthy process. Few believers become fully loving all at once. Charles engaged in a lively debate throughout the course of his life with his brother over this issue, in particular, and they never fully resolved their differences.[6] Charles always felt that John, primarily on the basis of his definitions, set the goal of sanctification too low, and John believed Charles set the bar too high. Over against John's more instantaneous view, Charles tended to emphasize God's gift of perfect love—the ultimate goal of the process of sanctification—in the moment of death. S T Kimbrough maintains that Charles "adamantly opposed the concepts of instantaneous perfection and instantaneous holiness and advocated a gradual pilgrimage toward perfection and holiness

---

5. We will explore these themes more fully in the final chapter of this book, on perfection.

6. On this issue, see Tyson, *Charles Wesley on Sanctification*, 227–301.

throughout one's life."[7] In a hymn on Hebrews 6:12 about patience he expresses his sentiments vehemently:

> Nature would the crown receive
> The first moment we believe,
> But we vainly think to seize
> Instantaneous holiness:
> Faith alone cannot suffice,
> Patience too must earn the prize,
> Both insure the promise given,
> Lead through perfect love to heaven.
> (*Scripture Hymns*, 2:355–56)

Charles holds to God's promise, nonetheless, and expresses his confidence in God's power to accomplish this great work over time. In the famous hymn entitled "The Promise of Sanctification," he defends this doctrine against its many detractors:

> Hast thou not said, who canst not lie,
>   That I thy law shall keep and do?
> Lord, I believe, though men deny.
>   They all are false, but thou art true. (46)

He talks frequently about continuing on towards the goal with calm zeal for the prize of the heavenly call of God in Christ Jesus. In one of his *Trinity Hymns* he simply proclaims, "Lord, we believe the promise sure . . . To keep us pure in life and heart" (38). And again:

> In Jesus we believe,
>   And wait the truth to prove,
> We shall, we shall receive
>   The blessing from above,
> Fullness of love, and peace, and power,
> And live in Christ, and sin no more. (*HSP 1749*, 2:328–29)

---

7. Kimbrough, *Lyrical Theology*, 105.

He reflects the same profound optimism in the power of God's grace in a reflection on Luke 18:1: "If I believe in thee, / Nothing is too hard for me" (*Scripture Hymns*, 2:230). Moving toward this goal entails growth in grace and love.

In a single-stanza hymn, Wesley reflects on a phrase from 1 Thessalonians 4:3: "For this is the will of God, your sanctification." He believed that God's deep desire is for everyone to become loving, to be holy. He also acknowledged that every person has a deep longing for this as well.

> He wills, that I should holy be:
>   That holiness I long to feel,
> That full divine conformity
>   To all my Savior's righteous will:
> See, Lord, the travail of your soul
>   Accomplished in the change of mine,
> And plunge me, every whit made whole,
>   In all the depths of love divine. (*Scripture Hymns*, 2:324)

Wesley's mysticism emerges in these closing lines. God's love is a mystery into which the children of God plunge themselves. In the second stanza of this hymn, originally written as a separate reflection on the story of the woman who was healed by touching the fringe of Jesus's robe (Matt 14:36), Wesley articulates the therapeutic nature of the process of sanctification. The juxtaposition of these two stanzas in the creation of a new hymn demonstrates the connection between holiness and healing. Growth in grace and love necessarily entails healing.

> Lord, I believe your power the same,
>   The same your truth and grace endure,
> And in your blessed hands I am,
>   And trust you for a perfect cure;
> Come, Savior, come, and make me whole,
>   Entirely all my sins remove,
> To perfect health restore my soul,
>   To perfect holiness and love. (*Scripture Hymns*, 2:169–70)

If the faithful have any hope of becoming loving and whole, God must remove all sin and restore their original capacity to love. Perfect health means to love as God loves.

Growth, in fact, characterizes all of life. Wesley believed that life in Christ should be no different. Given the relational character of Christianity, he intuited perhaps that growth toward the fullest possible love of God and others is proportional to the growth of the believer's trust in Christ. Charles was convinced that the more Christians love the more consistent their practice of love would become in their lives. The goal is for a Christian's loving to become "second nature" in the same way that the beating of the heart and breathing continue without interruption or deviation. The following hymn, titled "For a Tender Conscience," reflects these concerns. Wesley understood the importance of a habituated, internal guidance mechanism—developed over time—that functions as an arbiter of words and actions.

> I want a principle within
>   Of watchful, godly fear,
> A sensibility of sin,
>   A pain to feel it near.
> I want the first approach to feel
>   Of pride or wrong desire,
> To catch the wandering of my will,
>   And quench the kindling fire.
>
> From thee that I no more may stray,
>   No more thy goodness grieve,
> Grant me the filial awe, I pray,
>   The tender conscience give.
> Quick as the apple of an eye,
>   O God, my conscience make;
> Awake my soul when sin is nigh,
>   And keep it still awake. (*HSP 1749*, 2:230–31)

Wesley knew how important the cultivation of the conscience was for the maintenance of healthy and happy relationships, for growth in grace and love. Most importantly he was concerned that the early Methodist people develop a biblical understanding of how good and evil forces shape their decisions in life. Of particular concern to him was the seductive power of pride, wrong desire, and the wandering will, all antithetical to the loving mind that was in Christ. The process of growth in grace necessarily entails bringing unruly wills and passions under the control of a godly principle. It means fixing this principle at the very center of one's being, the source of all words and actions. It means testing every thought, word, and deed against the measure of God's love.

Means of Grace

Having placed such a high priority on growth in the Christian life toward the goal of perfect love, it was incumbent upon Charles to counsel the Methodists about the "how" of this process. His hymns proved to be potent instruments in teaching the Methodist people about practices that would enable them to grow in grace and love. Wesley firmly believed that Christians only grow when they immerse themselves in those spiritual practices in which God has promised to be present. Those practices that exerted the greatest influence in Charles's own life reflect the traditions and practices of the Anglican heritage he loved and emulated. This constellation of spiritual practices—what Charles and John called "means of grace"—included prayer and fasting, Bible study, Christian conference or fellowship, and participation in the sacrament of Holy Communion.[8] They described these as the "instituted means of grace" or "works of piety." Not only did these activities nurture and sustain growth in grace and love, they fueled the Wesleyan movement as a powerful religious awakening.

"[I] pressed the use of means [of grace], as means, from Isaiah 58," Charles recorded in his journal on October 27, 1739, "which is full of promises to those that walk in the ordinances with a sincere

---

8. See Chilcote, "Charles Wesley and Christian Practices," 35–47.

heart."[9] The months that followed were filled with controversy because of some who advised against engaging in these practices for fear of putting their trust in these "works" rather than in the grace of God. Charles could not abide this position and fought against it tooth and nail. Instead, he argued for the use of means because it was in the means that God had promised to meet the faithful. He made this perspective abundantly clear in his hymns. In a lengthy hymn titled "The Bloody Issue Cured" he confessed,

> But now I seek to touch my Lord,
> To hear his whisper in the word,
>   To feel his Spirit blow;
> To catch the love of which I read,
> To taste him in the mystic bread,
>   And all his sweetness know. (*HSP 1749*, 1:170)

His twenty-three-stanza hymn titled "The Means of Grace" encouraged the Methodist people to meet God in the means:

> Suffice for me, that thou, my Lord,
>   Hast bid me fast and pray:
> Thy will be done, thy name adored;
>   'Tis only mine to obey.
>
> Thou biddest me search the sacred leaves,
>   And taste the hallowed bread:
> The kind commands my soul receives,
>   And longs on thee to feed.
>
> Still for thy loving kindness, Lord,
>   I in thy temple wait;
> I look to find thee in thy word,
>   Or at thy table meet. (*HSP 1740*, 37)

Charles met Jesus in the means, and he taught that these means enable Christians to grow in grace and love.

9. Kimbrough and Newport, *Manuscript Journal*, 1:217.

Among the biblical themes in Charles's lyrical theology identified in this study, two means of grace stand out: prayer and sacrament. If Wesley had been asked how to sustain the journey of sanctification, he would easily have advised others to practice prayer and participate in the sacrament. We will explore these two themes in the next two chapters.

Questions for Consideration

1. What does the word *sanctification* mean?

2. What is the relationship of justification to sanctification?

3. How do Charles and John Wesley relate a "forensic" understanding of salvation and a "therapeutic" view of salvation in the journey toward redemption? How are they related, yet distinct?

4. How are the classical themes of *apophatic* (emptying) and *kataphatic* (filling) related to the indwelling of the Holy Spirit in the Christian life?

5. What is the ultimate goal of sanctification? Why did John Wesley feel Charles set the bar too high?

6. What is the connection between holiness and healing? What holds them together in Charles Wesley's lyrical theology?

7. What does Wesley mean by wanting a "principle within"? What is it?

8. What are the means of grace? What did the early Methodists believe about meeting God through them? How are growing in grace and practicing the means of grace related?

six

Prayer: Abiding in Christ

FOR CHARLES WESLEY PRAYER was a foundational means of grace. In his practice prayer informed all the other means of grace in one way or another—indeed, he viewed it as the bedrock of the Christian life. He learned the importance of a disciplined devotional life in the Epworth rectory, his childhood home, under the spiritual instruction of his mother, Susanna. Several features of the spirituality formed on his mother's knee are transparent in his lyrical corpus. (1) The seasons and cycles of the Christian Year framed his life of prayer. His *Resurrection, Ascension, Whitsunday,* and *Festival Hymns* (all published in 1746), as well as his earlier *Nativity Hymns* (1745), all draw attention to the saving work of God in Jesus Christ through an annual cycle of remembrance. Wesley composed hundreds of hymns that enabled the Methodist people to ponder the meaning of Jesus's life through this cycle of prayer and reflection. (2) Charles viewed prayer as a means of sharing sacred space with Jesus, of abiding with Christ. He set time aside to be with God, to nurture his relationship with God in Christ. (3) He prayed the scriptures. He found an inseparable connection between the Word and the life of prayer. The Word pervades the hymn-prayers of his *Collection.*

Three powerful words: "Pray without ceasing" (1 Thess 5:17). Wesley provided a lyrical paraphrase of this signature biblical text in his *Scripture Hymns* of 1762, and it sets the tone for this chapter on prayer:

> Father, into my heart convey
> The power incessantly to pray,
>   Or thy command is void:
> But when the power inhabits there,
> My heart shall be an house of prayer,
>   Emptied, and filled with God. (2:325)

Wesley viewed the Christian life as *via devotio* (a way of devotion). In his lyrical theology he often described the heart of the Christian as a house of prayer. He endeavored in his own personal life and encouraged all Methodists to cultivate the practice of prayer as one of the most important components of the spiritual journey. He viewed prayer as a fundamental means of grace that enables the disciple of Jesus to grow in grace and love. But he also acknowledged that only God can supply the power to fulfill God's own command. In this chapter we will explore prayer as a critical practice related to Christian discipleship and Charles's doctrine of prayer.

In his lyrical exposition of the whole armor of God (Eph 6)—the signature hymn for prayer—Charles includes the following reflection on St. Paul's admonition:

> Pray, without ceasing pray
> (Your Captain gives the word),
> His summons cheerfully obey,
>   And call upon the Lord;
>   To God your every want
>   In instant prayer display;
> Pray always; pray, and never faint;
>   Pray, without ceasing pray.

In fellowship, alone,
  To God with faith draw near,
Approach God's courts, besiege God's throne
    With all the powers of prayer.
    Go to God's temple, go,
    Nor from God's altar move;
Let every house God's worship know,
    And every heart God's love.

    Pour out your souls to God,
    And bow them with your knees,
And spread your hearts and hands abroad,
    And pray for Sion's peace;
    Your fellow pilgrims bear
    Forever on your mind;
Extend the arms of mighty prayer,
    Ingrasping humankind. (*HSP 1749*, 1:238–39)

This hymn identifies several critical elements related to prayer in addition to the claim for the need of constancy. Charles connects the practice immediately with the heart. He describes the posture of the soul in relation to God: bowed, open, extended. He concludes the hymn with a powerful expression. By means of prayer, the Christian community "ingrasps" all humankind. The prayers of the faithful unite them with others and receive those who are outside the community of faith into their embrace. Prayer not only unites the believer with God and feeds the soul but also connects those who pray with other people in ways that are meant to be healing and life-giving. Charles's hymns promote Jesus's own practice of prayer—a model that entails a particular pattern and a commitment to discipline.

The Model and Teaching of Jesus

Jesus's Practice

In a sermon based on John 8 Charles explicitly teaches his hearers to follow the pattern of Jesus in their life of prayer: "*Jesus went unto the Mount of Olives; and early in the morning he came again into the Temple.* The life of Christ is the life of Christians; who, if they are Christians indeed, walk as He also walked, spending their time in works of piety and charity, on the Mount or with the multitude. From prayer they return with their Lord to doing good, from do-ing good they retire to prayer. Each fits the other; retirement for action, and action for retirement." Charles often describes Jesus as a "praying pattern." A continuous rhythm of time apart with God and engagement with people, dealing with the real concerns of their lives, characterized his own spirituality. He drew his energy for ministry and mission from his time of communion with God. Charles's hymn "For a family of believers" provides a portrait of Jesus's prayer pattern:

> Early in the temple met
>   Let us still our Maker greet,
> Nightly to the mount repair,
>   Join our praying pattern there.
>
> There by wrestling faith obtain
>   Power to work for God again,
> Power God's image to retrieve,
>   Power like thee our Lord to live. (*Family Hymns*, 42)

Wesley draws his primary image of Jesus's life of prayer from the event of the Transfiguration recorded in Luke 9, a story that underscores this rhythm of contemplation and action. From his mountaintop experience he descends into the valley of life where he is immediately confronted with a sick child whom he heals. This is the pattern of Jesus's life throughout the Gospels—from com-munion with God to mission in the world. In imitation of Christ, believers capture glimpses of the glory of God on the mountaintop of prayer and then love and serve others for God's glory in the enactment of prayer in life. Charles provides a lyrical description of this pattern of *ora et labora* (prayer and labor—contemplation and action):

> Vessels, instruments of grace,
>> Pass we thus our happy days
> 'Twixt the mount and multitude,
>> Doing or receiving good.
>
> Glad to pray and labor on,
>> Till our earthly course is run,
> Till we on the sacred tree
>> Bow the head and die like thee. (*Family Hymns,* 42)

True prayer moves the disciple to action based on the pattern of Jesus. It does not confront the seeker with ideas; it builds a relationship with the ultimate, personal reality of the universe—the Triune God. Prayer, in Charles's view, entails listening and speaking heart to heart and then turning that conversation into loving action.

Jesus's Prayer

Not only Jesus's practice, but the prayer he taught his disciples—the Lord's Prayer—provides a starting point in the quest for a cultivated life of prayer for Wesley. The *Collection* includes a nine-stanza lyrical paraphrase of the Lord's Prayer, but it is from the pen of John. Nevertheless, Charles alludes to or directly quotes the longer version of the prayer (Matt 6:9–13) twenty-three times.[1] Three out of four of these references allude to the petition "Thy kingdom come, Thy will be done in earth, as it is in heaven" (6:10). For Charles, this is the primary lens; God's rule and will dominate his vision of prayer through the prism of this particular prayer.

---

1. There are hardly any references to the short form of the prayer in Luke 11:2–4.

Since we will explore this aspect of Charles's theology in a subsequent chapter on "dominion," several comments suffice here.

Matthew 6:10 inspired these words:

> Jesu, the life, the truth, the way,
>> In whom I now believe,
> As taught by thee, in faith I pray,
>> Expecting to receive.
>
> Thy will by me on earth be done,
>> As by the choirs above,
> Who always see thee on thy throne,
>> And glory in thy love. (*HSP 1742*, 230)

Two important aspects of Charles's theology of prayer surface in these stanzas. First, God not only hears but answers prayer. Second, believers not only pray for God to accomplish God's will, they become partners in the establishment of God's rule. Charles emphasizes both God's faithfulness and human responsibility. Another hymn in which Wesley alludes to this petition, entitled "An Hourly Act of Oblation," paints a poignant portrait of the believer at prayer:

> God of almighty love,
>> By whose sufficient grace
> I lift my heart to things above,
>> And humbly seek thy face;
>> Through Jesus Christ the just
>> My faint desires receive,
> And let me in thy goodness trust,
>> And to thy glory live.
>
> Whate'er I speak, or do,
>> Thy glory be my aim:
> My offerings all are offered through
>> The ever-blessed name:
>> Jesus, my single eye

Is fixed on thee alone,
Thy name be praised on earth, on high,
Thy will by all be done. (*HSP 1749*, 1:251–52)

The Christian prays to God through Jesus Christ. Christians fulfill God's will by virtue of a "single eye"—by remaining fixed on Jesus.

The Discipline of Prayer

Prayer, like every means of grace, requires discipline. Unless the followers of Jesus pray ceaselessly, Wesley believed, they will never uncover their true selves. God's glory will never be able to shine through them fully.

I want a heart to pray,
To pray and never cease,
Never to murmur at thy stay,
Or wish my sufferings less.

This blessing above all,
Always to pray I want,
Out of the deep on thee to call,
And never, never faint. (*HSP 1742*, 147–48)

God's prior faithfulness establishes a foundation for the faithfulness of the disciple of Jesus. Despite repeated failure and lack of faithfulness on the part of God's children, God always remains faithful.

Jesu, my strength, my hope,
On you I cast my care,
With humble confidence look up,
And know you hear my prayer.

Give me on you to wait
Till I can all things do,
On you, Almighty, to create,
Almighty to renew. (*HSP 1742*, 146–47)

But God's children wait for God not by doing nothing; rather, they must immerse themselves in this means of grace where God has promised to meet them. For Charles this was a daily regimen.

Throughout the course of his life Charles began every day with Morning Prayer and ended every day with Evening Prayer from the Anglican *Book of Common Prayer*. This practice in and of itself may have formed his spirituality more than any other influence. Praying these set forms of prayer daily meant that he recited the entire Psalter on a regular basis. The Psalms became his principal songbook. A rich collection of so-called "Office Hymns," mostly drawn from scripture, like the *Magnificat* and the *Sursum corda*, shaped his vision of faith. These prayers became part of his lyrical repertoire. No doubt, extemporaneous prayer shaped Charles's intimate relationship with God, but so did the great prayers of the church, such as the *Te Deum*. His lyrical reformulation of this great act of praise is masterful:

> When thou hadst all thy foes o'ercome,
> Returning to thy glorious home
> Thou didst receive the full reward,
> That I might share it with my Lord,
> And thus thine own new name obtain,
> And one with thee forever reign. (*Scripture Hymns*, 2:421)

Set forms of prayer shaped his theology, and he articulated this doctrine through the hymns.

Prayer in the 1780 *Collection*

Wesley explicitly devotes five sections of the *Collection* to the practice of prayer as it relates to blessing (Part 1, Section 3), repentance (Part 3, Section 1), believers praying (Part 4, Section 3), believers interceding for the world (Part 4, Section 9), and societies praying (Part 5, Section 3). The hymns included in these sections—nearly one hundred—constitute almost 20 percent of the collection, demonstrating the preeminent place of prayer in Charles's theology.

Moreover, the majority of the hymns Wesley wrote are, in fact, prayers in themselves. The first two sections reflect Charles's emphasis on the way of salvation, while the latter sections provide a balanced vision of individual and corporate practices of prayer and the need to intercede for others and the world.

Blessing

Charles focuses particular attention in this section on prayer that awakens and redeems the fallen child of God. "Fill every soul with sacred grief," the singer prays, "and then with sacred peace" (*HSP 1749*, 1:319). The Lord "impoverishes" and then "relieves," imparts a sense of guilt and then removes the load. "The knowledge of our sickness give, / The knowledge of our cure." In "Spirit of Faith Come Down" (*HPT*, 30–31) the singer prays first for revelation: "Spirit of faith come down, / reveal the things of God." Secondly, the singer prays for true acknowledgment. The Spirit of Love enables the creature to recognize the futility of the human way, removes the veil between the human and the divine, and provides the capacity to envisage God's reign. Thirdly, the singer prays for the redemption of all: "O that the world might know / The all-atoning Lamb." Fourthly, the singer prays for new birth. Prayer can inspire a living faith as the Spirit's great gift. It conquers all and leads to perfect love. Reflecting on this hymn, S T Kimbrough observes, "'O that the world might know' that it can grow in love and peace instead of hatred and war. Such a worldwide regeneration, new birth, or new beginning is the hope of the descent of the Spirit of love which God pours into our hearts."[2]

Repentance

The primary theme of this section is that which we explored fully in chapter 3 on the contrite heart. Many of the hymns quoted in that chapter, as we saw, come from this section of the *Collection*. In these hymns Charles provides a lyrical explication of prayer for "a

---

2. Kimbrough, *Heart to Praise My God*, 175.

clean heart" and "renewal of spirit." Every selection in this section is a hymn-prayer addressed either to God or to Jesus the Savior. The closing stanza of the opening hymn for this section articulates Wesley's pathos around this theme:

> Ah, give me, Lord, myself to feel,
> My total misery reveal;
> Ah, give me, Lord (I still would say),
> A heart to mourn, a heart to pray;
> My business this, my only care,
> My life, my every breath be prayer![3]

Lamentation characterizes these hymns; the sinner's prayer—*kyrie eleison*—pervades Charles's texts: "Groan the sinner's only plea, / God, be merciful to me!" (*HSP* 1749, 1:74).

Believers Praying

"Desiring to Pray," the opening hymn of the section "For Believers Praying," could be described as a "prayer before prayer."[4] In this magisterial hymn Wesley reaches from the first to the last chapter of the Bible and weaves throughout the poetic structure the central theme of prayer. In the first stanza he invites the sovereign Lord to "instruct us how to pray!" Having confessed the inability of the creature to pray, in verse 2 he pleads, "And send us down the Comforter; / The Spirit of ceaseless prayer impart." He then affirms that only the Spirit can "make our heart a house of prayer." The hymn concludes thus:

> Come in thy pleading Spirit down
>   To us who for thy coming stay;
> Of all thy gifts we ask but one—
>   We ask the constant power to pray;
> Indulge us, Lord, in this request!

3. Attributed by some to John and not Charles Wesley, this hymn titled "A Prayer under Convictions" comes from *HSP* 1739, 85–86.

4. See Hildebrandt and Beckerlegge, *Collection*, 436; see *HSP* 1749, 2:35–37.

Thou canst not then deny the rest.

Wesley establishes an inseparable connection between those who pray and the Spirit. Throughout this hymn Charles uses the first person plural. "The joint complaint" and "the common want" dominate, rather than the angst of the individual. But Wesley's "pray *we* on" often alternates with "bid *me* turn again." The community prays both "me" and "we." The language itself reflects his conviction that prayer is both an individual and a social practice.

Several themes characterize the eleven hymns of this section, including the centrality of the heart and the power of prayer, but Charles roots the primary theme in a biblical narrative, namely, the parable of the persistent widow in Luke 18:1–8. He alludes to or quotes this text more than any other in these hymns. This story emphasizes the need to pray continuously and not to be discouraged. In another hymn entitled "Desiring to Pray" (*HSP 1749*, 2:38–39), Charles provides a lyrical paraphrase of the parable. Every stanza concludes with the words, "Pray we, every moment pray, / And never, never faint." The hymn not only counsels constant prayer; it is also a diatribe against those who promoted a "doctrine of stillness." In 1740, the Wesleys broke from a group of radical Moravians who argued that seekers should abstain from all means of grace. Since salvation came through the gift of faith, they argued, and nothing could be done to earn it, then those who sought faith should simply wait for it and do absolutely nothing. They should be still. Charles retaliated in verse:

> Place no longer let us give
>   To the old tempter's will,
> Nevermore our duty leave
>   While Satan cries, "Be still!"
> Stand we in the ancient way,
> And here with God ourselves acquaint:
>   Pray we, every moment pray,
>   And never, never faint.

The practice of prayer, Charles insisted, remains the duty even of those who love God and neighbor in the fullest possible way: "Pray we on when all-renewed / And perfected in love."

Believers Interceding

The Wesley brothers encouraged their people to gather once a week, usually at noon on Fridays, to share in intercessory prayer.[5] In 1758 Charles published a collection of forty hymns devoted to intercessory concerns ranging from childbirth to war. A number of these hymns can be found among the thirty-seven hymns "For Believers Interceding for the World" in the *Collection*. Charles placed great importance on this corporate practice. He called upon Methodists to intercede for people of other faiths, his primary concern being the universal preaching of the gospel:

> Art thou the God of Jews alone,
>   And not the God of Gentiles too?
> To Gentiles make thy goodness known,
>   Thy judgments to the nations show;
> Awake them by the gospel call—
> Light of the world, illumine all! (*Intercession Hymns*, 28)

Through these intercessory hymns Methodists prayed for England and the king, for peace in the midst of war, for the fallen and lost, for parents and children. "Savior, to thee we humbly cry," they prayed. "The brethren we have lost restore" (*HSP 1749*, 2:102). "O let the prisoners' mournful cries," they pled, "as incense in thy sight appear!" (*HSP 1749*, 2:90). The community had particular concern for those being baptized. They sang them into the new reality that they hoped would characterize their lives:

> Let the promised inward grace
>   Accompany the sign;
> On her new-born soul impress
>   The glorious name divine:
> Father, all thy love reveal,

5. See Kimbrough and Newport, *Manuscript Journal*, 1:268 (June 13, 1740).

> Jesus all thy mind impart,
> Holy Ghost, renew, and dwell
> Forever in her heart! (*HSP 1749*, 2:246)

Societies Praying

This final section devoted specifically to prayer constitutes another large collection of thirty-nine hymns. Like the intercession hymns, these lyrical prayers are wide-ranging, including themes such as family, friendship, mutual support, unity, and the communion of saints. Charles expresses a number of these common elements in a stanza from his extended hymn for the love-feast:

> Let us join ('tis God commands),
> Let us join our hearts and hands;
> Help to gain our calling's hope,
> Build we each the other up.
>
> God his blessing shall dispense,
> God shall crown his ordinance,
> Meet in his appointed ways,
> Nourish us with social grace. (*HSP 1740*, 183)

This ultimate concept about "social grace" pervades the hymns; Charles's phrases "to help each other on" and "hand in hand go on" articulate his vision of solidarity, camaraderie, and unity in the community of faith. He provides multiple lyrical commentaries on the Wesleyan theme of "watching over one another in love."

> Whate'er thou dost on one bestow,
> Let each the doubled blessing know,
>   Let each the common burden bear;
> In comforts and in griefs agree,
> And wrestle for his friend with thee
>   In all the omnipotence of prayer.
> Our mutual prayer accept and seal! (*HSP 1749*, 2:265)

Sacred Song as Prayer

If St. Augustine was right in his claim that "to sing is to pray twice," Charles and the early Methodist people did a lot of praying! Singing praise to God transforms the singer. Those Christians who sing their prayers connect with God in ways beyond explanation. Sacred song as prayer shapes the people of God. Charles's hymn-prayers often epitomize the quest for intimacy with God:

> O thou who camest from above
>   The pure celestial fire to impart,
> Kindle a flame of sacred love
>   On the mean altar of my heart!
> There let it for thy glory burn
>   With inextinguishable blaze,
> And trembling to its source return
>   In humble love, and fervent praise.
>
> Jesu, confirm my heart's desire
>   To work, and speak, and think for thee;
> Still let me guard the holy fire,
>   And still stir up thy gift in me;
> Ready for all thy perfect will,
>   My acts of faith and love repeat,
> Till death thy endless mercies seal,
>   And make the sacrifice complete. (*Scripture Hymns*, 1:57)

This hymn describes Charles's vision of inward religion perfectly. Despite the purposeful cultivation of the practice of prayer in life—something essential to growth in the grace and love of God and others—Charles placed the highest level of importance on attentive abiding in Christ. The ultimate goal of the spiritual quest, he believed, is a heartfelt desire for God's presence to transform every person into a Christlike child of God. In prayer the disciple experiences this presence. Charles also experienced this presence in the sacrament of Holy Communion—the second means of grace we will examine—and his doctrine of the Lord's Supper reveals some of his most critical theological convictions.

Questions for Consideration

1. How does Charles Wesley view the life of prayer?

2. What biblical images and passages does Wesley employ to describe the life of prayer?

3. How do Wesley's hymns speak of Jesus's own practice of prayer?

4. In what ways does Wesley use the Lord's Prayer in Matthew's Gospel as a lens through which to understand prayer?

5. What theological resources does Charles Wesley utilize to enrich the life and discipline of prayer among the Methodists? How does his own Anglican heritage shape his outlook and practice of prayer as a means of grace?

6. How does Wesley divide the sections on prayer in his 1780 *Collection* of poetry and hymns? How does Wesley incorporate the disciplines of prayer collectively and individually among the early Methodists? What biblical themes permeate these sections?

7. How does the corporate nature of prayer in Wesley's lyrical theology speak to the concept of "social grace" as "watching out over one another in love"? How are prayer and singing related?

seven

Communion: Spiritual Food for the Journey

CHARLES WESLEY DESCRIBED THE sacrament of the Lord's Supper, Eucharist, or Holy Communion as the "richest legacy" that Jesus left the community of faith. In 1745 he jointly published *Hymns on the Lord's Supper* with his brother.[1] This collection of 166 hymns, perhaps the most significant corpus of English poetry devoted to sacramental theology, demonstrates the centrality of the Eucharist to Wesleyan spirituality. Charles's signature hymn on the sacrament, drawn from this collection, explores the many dimensions of this ritual sign-act of love for the Christian community:

> Fasting he doth and hearing bless,
>   And prayer can much avail,
> Good vessels all to draw the grace
>   Out of salvation's well.

---

1. Two monumental studies of this hymn collection provide a panoramic vision of Charles Wesley's eucharistic theology: Rattenbury, *Eucharistic Hymns*, and Stevick, *Altar's Fire*. All hymns quoted in this chapter are cited from *HLS* unless otherwise noted.

But none like this mysterious rite
  Which dying mercy gave
Can draw forth all God's promised might
  And all God's will to save.

This is the richest legacy
  Thou hast on us bestowed,
Here chiefly, Lord, we feed on thee,
  And drink thy precious blood.

Here all thy blessings we receive,
  Here all thy gifts are given;
To those that would in thee believe,
  Pardon, and grace, and heaven.

Thus may we still in thee be blessed
  Till all from earth remove,
And share with thee the marriage feast,
  And drink the wine above. (31)

Constant Communion

Scholars have documented the general neglect of the sacrament in the Church of England at the outset of the Wesleyan revival in the eighteenth century. While many acknowledge the Wesleys' movement of renewal as a great awakening of faith, less is known about the critical role the Wesleys played in reviving eucharistic practice in the Church; the Wesleyan revival was both evangelical and sacramental. In stark contrast to the norms of his age, Charles helped put the sacrament back at the very center of Christian spirituality and discipleship, and his hymns played a significant role in these developments. The personal practice of the Wesleys in this regard—both Charles and John—influenced the lives of the early Methodist people in remarkable ways. John Bowmer's detailed study of early Methodist sacramental practice demonstrates just how central the Lord's Supper was to their understanding of the faith: "There can be little doubt that the high place which the sacrament occupied in early Methodism was due to the precept and the example of the Wesleys, for it is not too much to say that for them it was the highest form of devotion and the most comprehensive act of worship the Church could offer. As necessary as preaching was—and it would be unjust to attempt to minimize its place in the Methodist revival—a preaching service was not, to the Wesleys, the supreme spiritual exercise. On the other hand, the Lord's Supper was completely satisfying."[2] The evidence concerning the lives of both brothers demonstrates two facts: (1) their frequent participation in the sacrament and their practice, in general, remained remarkably consistent over the course of their lives; and (2) they either celebrated or participated in Eucharist on every possible occasion, frequently more often than once a week.

Two documents among Charles's works carry the title "Constant Communion." The first is a discursive defense of the sacrament; the second is a monumental sacred poem. The primary purpose of both was to demonstrate the duty of every Christian to receive the Lord's Supper as often as possible—in other words, to practice constant Communion. He concludes the brief prose document arguing for the celebration of the Lord's Supper every Sunday because "both Scripture and tradition do give plain evidence for the necessity of making at least a weekly oblation of the Christian sacrifice, and of honouring every Lord's Day with a solemn public celebration of the Lord's Supper."[3] A twenty-two stanza poem concludes the *Hymns on the Lord's Supper* and laments the decline of vitality in the church, noting a critical reason for its deterioration:

> Why is the faithful seed decreased,
>   The life of God extinct and dead?
> The daily sacrifice is ceased,
>   And charity to heaven is fled. (140)

2. Bowmer, *Lord's Supper in Early Methodism*, 188–89.
3. "Sermon 13: Acts 20:7," in Newport, *Sermons*, 286.

Charles implores God to restore the daily celebration of the meal and laments the way its neglect has quenched the spark of love among the faithful.

In Charles's poem "Come to the feast, for Christ invites," as Kimbrough observes, "he goes one step further in his argument for 'constant communion.' He believes strongly that no one has the right to determine the non-necessity of the Eucharist."[4]

> 'Tis not for us to set our God
> A time his grace to give,
> The benefit whene'er bestowed
> We gladly should receive. (44)

Why would anyone not want to experience God's grace and love, union with Christ, all the life of God, and the visitation of the Holy Spirit as often as possible? Why would they absent themselves from this promised place of divine-human encounter? The Wesleys and the early Methodists flocked to the celebration of Holy Communion quite simply because they encountered God there, which led them to view the Lord's Supper as the "chief means of grace." In his *Hymns on the Lord's Supper* Charles gives a primary place to the sacrament among the various means of grace in which believers meet the Triune God and are nurtured in their faith-filled relationship with Christ:

> The prayer, the fast, the word conveys,
> When mixed with faith, thy life to me,
> In all the channels of thy grace,
> I still have fellowship with thee,
> But chiefly here my soul is fed
> With fullness of immortal bread. (39)

Most tables signify meals, and those who gather around the Lord's Table received spiritual nourishment there. These "feasts of love," as the early Methodists often described them, shaped their understanding of God's love for them and their reciprocal love for God.

---

4. Kimbrough, "Charles Wesley's Understanding of the Church," 140.

Eucharistic Theology

While the Wesley brothers jointly published *Hymns on the Lord's Supper*, Charles wrote virtually all the 166 hymns in this unique volume. This collection of religious verse comprises the fullest possible expression of his eucharistic doctrine—a theology in hymns. "The eighteenth-century revival," Richard Heitzenrater observed, "was to a great extent borne on the wings of Charles's poetry. Charles's hymns not only helped form the texture of the Methodist mind but also, perhaps more importantly, set the temper of the Methodist spirit."[5] Nothing could be more true of Methodist eucharistic faith and practice.

This collection of eucharistic hymns included John's abridged version of Daniel Brevint's *Christian Sacrament and Sacrifice*, which functioned as a preface to the volume. John most likely arranged Charles's hymns under primary headings, closely following the pattern established by Brevint in his treatise:

1. As it is a Memorial of the Sufferings and Death of Christ.

2. As it is a Sign and a Means of Grace.

3. The Sacrament a Pledge of Heaven.

4. The Holy Eucharist as it implies a Sacrifice.

5. Concerning the Sacrifice of our Persons.

6. After the Sacrament.

The first three sections closely parallel the dimensions of time and provide the outline for Charles's lyrical theological reflections on the sacrament as a memorial (the past), a sign and means of grace (the present), and a pledge of heaven (the future). Theological concerns about the sacrament and sacrifice (the fourth and fifth sections of the collection), Christ's presence, and eschatological hope parallel each of these time dimensions, respectively.

5. Quoted in Kimbrough, *Lost in Wonder*, 11–12.

The Lord's Supper: Memorial and Sacrifice

The Lord's Supper is a memorial of the passion of Christ. The opening hymn of Wesley's collection sets the somber tone of this section:

> In that sad memorable night,
>   When Jesus was for us betrayed,
> He left his death-recording rite,
>   He took, and blessed, and broke the bread,
> And gave his own their last bequest,
> And thus his love's intent expressed:
>
> Take eat, this is my body given,
>   To purchase life and peace for you,
> Pardon and holiness and heaven;
>   Do this, my dying love to show,
> Accept your precious legacy,
> And thus, my friends, remember me. (1)

The sacrament proclaims "the Lord's death until he comes," St. Paul reminded the Corinthian community (1 Cor 11:26). Charles's death imagery in these "past dimension hymns," therefore, should be no surprise. The fact that the redemptive suffering of Jesus procures eternal life for the believer, however, startles those who experience the power of this redemptive act of love:

> The grace which I to all bequeath
>   In this divine memorial take,
> And mindful of your Savior's death,
>   Do this, my followers, for my sake,
> Whose dying love hath left behind
> Eternal life for all mankind. (2)

As critical as this memorial aspect is for Wesley, he recoils from a "bare memorialism" in his view of the sacrament. Rather, sacramental remembrance connotes *anamnesis*, that is, calling an event to mind in such a way as to make it real in the present moment.

Memory has always functioned in this way for the Hebrew people in the annual remembrance of Passover. Jewish families celebrate the Passover meal not simply to recall God's deliverance of the people of Israel from bondage in Egypt but to experience liberation in the present moment as well. Charles's masterful "Protestant crucifix" hymn, quoted above as an illustration of his theology of the cross, bears repeating here to demonstrate how his poetry brings Jesus's self-sacrifice to the forefront of the singers' consciousness and into their present experience at the table.

> Endless scenes of wonder rise
>   With that mysterious tree,
> Crucified before our eyes
>   Where we our Maker see:
> Jesus, Lord, what hast thou done!
>   Publish we the death divine,
> Stop, and gaze, and fall, and own
>   Was never love like thine!
>
> Never love nor sorrow was
>   Like that my Jesus showed;
> See him stretched on yonder cross
>   And crushed beneath our load!
> Now discern the deity,
>   Now his heavenly birth declare!
> Faith cries out, 'Tis he, 'tis he,
>   My God that suffers there! (16)

The sacrificial metaphors that Charles applied to the Lord's Supper are those which the writers of Hebrews and Revelation, in particular, employ most frequently—the slaughtered Lamb who was also the great high priest. This priest-victim imagery brings out with unequivocal force Wesley's sense of the continuing power of sacrifice on the part of the ascended Christ. The cross not only represents the finished work of Christ on earth but points to the

Savior's continuing intercession on behalf of all. The priest-victim pleads the cause of sinful children for whom he died:

> Live our eternal priest
> By men and angels blest!
> Jesus Christ, the crucified,
> He who did for all atone,
> From the cross where once he died
> Now he up to heaven is gone.

> He ever lives, and prays
> For all the faithful race;
> In the holiest place above
> Sinners' advocate he stands,
> Pleads for us his dying love,
> Shows for us his bleeding hands. (100)

The sacrifice on which God is asked to look is not our own but the one oblation of Christ for the sins of the world—the sacrifice of God's beloved Son.

The sacrifice offered in the sacrament, however, also belongs to the faithful who join their sacrifice to Christ's. The sacrament refers not only to the dynamic sacrifice of Christ but reminds the community of faith—the church—of its obligation to engage in self-sacrificing acts of love in imitation of Christ. "Would the Savior of mankind / Without his people die?" Charles asks. "No, to him we all are joined / As more than standers by" (111). In a galloping hymn he describes the depth of solidarity with Christ that the believers experience in the sacrament:

> Shall we let our God groan
> And suffer alone,
> Or to Calvary fly,
> And nobly resolve with our Master to die!

> His servants shall be
> With him on the tree,

Where Jesus was slain,
His crucified servants shall always remain. (120)

Charles describes this sacrificial character of the Christian life, in which the worshiper participates repeatedly at the table of the Lord, and clarifies its relationship to the sacrifice of Christ:

While faith the atoning blood applies,
Ourselves a living sacrifice
  We freely offer up to God:
And none but those his glory share
Who crucified with Jesus are,
  And follow where their Savior trod.

Savior, to thee our lives we give,
Our meanest sacrifice receive,
  And to thy own oblation join,
Our suffering and triumphant head,
Through all thy states thy members lead,
  And seat us on the throne divine. (110)

The followers of Jesus offer up to God all their thoughts, words, and actions through the crucified Son as a sacrifice of praise and thanksgiving. Participation in the sacrament mandates that all take up the cross, thereby permitting God to form them into cruciform followers of the Lamb through the power of the Spirit.

Eucharist: Sign of Grace and Presence

The Eucharist is a celebration of the presence of the living Christ. Wesley associates this present dimension most closely with the sacrament as a "sign and means" of grace. Without any question, the earliest eucharistic feasts of the Christian community, at which the disciples of Jesus "ate their food with glad and generous hearts" (Acts 2:46), were characterized by joy and thanksgiving. Charles Wesley captured that primitive spirit of *eucharistia* or thanksgiving:

Jesu, we thus obey
Thy last and kindest word,
Here in thine own appointed way
We come to meet our Lord;
The way thou hast enjoined
Thou wilt therein appear:
We come with confidence to find
Thy special presence here.

Our hearts we open wide
To make the Savior room:
And lo! the Lamb, the crucified,
The sinner's friend, is come!
His presence makes the feast,
And now our bosoms feel
The glory not to be expressed,
The joy unspeakable. (69)

Charles believed that the outward sign transmits the signified through faith. Those who believe meet Jesus at the table, and the heights to which faith can move them are immeasurable:

The joy is more unspeakable,
And yields me larger draughts of God,
Till nature faints beneath the power,
And faith filled up can hold no more. (39)

The sacrament, according to Wesley, effects what it represents. According to Rattenbury, "an examination of the hymns will result quite frequently in the discovery of allusions to the 'real Presence' of Christ, but it is always a *personal* Presence."[6]

O thou who this mysterious bread
Didst in Emmaus break,
Return herewith our souls to feed,
And to thy followers speak.

6. Rattenbury, *Eucharistic Hymns*, 59.

Unseal the volume of thy grace,
  Apply the gospel-word;
Open our eyes to see thy face,
  Our hearts to know the Lord.

Of thee we commune still, and mourn
  Till thou the veil remove;
Talk with us, and our hearts shall burn
  With flames of fervent love.

Enkindle now the heavenly zeal,
  And make thy mercy known,
And give our pardoned souls to feel
  That God and love are one. (22–23)

While advocating what could be described with integrity as a "real presence," Wesley denied any position approaching "transubstantiation," the medieval dogma that asserted that the essence of the bread and wine are transformed into the essence of Christ's body and blood in the sacrament. Over against this more ancient view of real presence, Ole Borgen described the Wesleyan concept of real presence as a "dynamic" or "living presence," affirming that "wherever God acts, there God is."[7] Essentially, in one of his greatest hymns on eucharistic theology, Charles declared the depths of a holy mystery beyond the possibility of rational explanation:

O the depth of love divine,
  The unfathomable grace!
Who shall say how bread and wine
  God into man conveys?
How the bread his flesh imparts,
  How the wine transmits his blood,
Fills his faithful people's hearts
  With all the life of God!

7. See Borgen, *John Wesley on the Sacraments*, 58–69.

Let the wisest mortal show
  How we the grace receive:
Feeble elements bestow
  A power not theirs to give:
Who explains the wondrous way?
  How through these the virtue came?
These the virtue did convey,
  Yet still remain the same.

Sure and real is the grace,
  The manner be unknown;
Only meet us in thy ways
  And perfect us in one,
Let us taste the heavenly powers,
  Lord, we ask for nothing more;
Thine to bless, 'tis only ours
  To wonder, and adore. (41)

Holy Communion: Pledge of Heaven and Hope

Holy Communion is a pledge of the heavenly banquet to come. The holy meal anticipates the glorious reunion of the faithful at the heavenly feast. As the writer to the Hebrews claimed, "We are surrounded by a great cloud of witnesses" (12:1), and during the celebration of the sacrament the faithful become more fully aware of the presence of these sainted ones who have preceded them in the journey. Charles spoke often of the sacrament as a foretaste of this banquet, an earnest or pledge of things to come. "Title to eternal bliss / Here his precious death we find," he exclaimed. "This the pledge the earnest this / Of the purchased joys behind" (89). His rediscovery of a vital sense of the "communion of the saints" in relationship to this Holy Communion was a significant contribution that he made to the sacramental theology of his own day. Hope became the keynote of this future dimension of the sacrament in Wesley's eucharistic hymns.

"By faith and hope already there," sings Charles, "ev'n now the marriage-feast we share" (82). This is a "soul-transporting feast" that "bears us now on eagles' wings" and seals "our eternal bliss" (82–83). The amazing imagery in Charles's lyrical theology reflects his vision of the church as a community of hope:

> How glorious is the life above
>   Which in this ordinance we *taste*;
> That fullness of celestial love,
>   That joy which shall forever last!
>
> The light of life eternal darts
>   Into our souls a dazzling ray,
> A drop of heaven o'erflows our hearts,
>   And deluges the house of clay.
>
> Sure pledge of ecstasies unknown
>   Shall this divine communion be,
> The ray shall rise into a sun,
>   The drop shall swell into a sea. (87)

The Great Supper (Luke 14:15–23)

Wesley employed these various dimensions and explored this wide range of sacramental imagery in an effort to communicate the depth and breadth of meaning in the sacrament and to enrich the experience of the participants. In this sign-act of love, the past, present, and future—faith, hope, and love—are compressed, as it were, into a timeless, communal act of praise. Charles embraces the cross of Christ and urges the followers of Jesus to adopt a cruciform style of life in imitation of their Lord. He celebrates the presence of the living Lord, who calls everyone to his feast, and anticipates the mystery and wonder of a heavenly banquet at which God gathers the faithful around a table of love. The fullness of the Christian faith is celebrated in the mystery of a holy meal and the people of God are empowered to faithful ministry and service. As faithful disciples repeatedly participate in the eucharistic actions of taking, blessing, breaking, and giving—the constitutive elements of an authentic, sacrificial life—God conforms them to the image of Christ.

Charles composed a twenty-four stanza lyrical paraphrase of Jesus's parable of the great supper in Luke 14:15–23, the signature biblical text for the theme of communion.[8]

> Then Jesus said to him, "Someone gave a great dinner and invited many. At the time for the dinner he sent his slave to say to those who had been invited, 'Come; for everything is ready now.' But they all alike began to make excuses. The first said to him, 'I have bought a piece of land, and I must go out and see it; please accept my apologies.' Another said, 'I have bought five yoke of oxen, and I am going to try them out; please accept my apologies.' Another said, 'I have just been married, and therefore I cannot come.' So the slave returned and reported this to his master. Then the owner of the house became angry and said to his slave, 'Go out at once into the streets and lanes of the town and bring in the poor, the crippled, the blind, and the lame.' And the slave said, 'Sir, what you ordered has been done, and there is still room.' Then the master said to the slave, 'Go out into the roads and lanes, and compel people to come in, so that my house may be filled.'"

First published in *Redemption Hymns* (1747), this hymn presents his idea of the inclusive nature of God's dominion. It sounds a note of eschatological urgency with regard to the ultimate victory of God's inclusive love. God invites all to the table. God offers grace to every soul. God excludes none from the gracious offer of life under God's loving rule. Wesley paints a compelling and dynamic

---

8. While this is not a text that occurs with great frequency in the *Collection*, I have taken liberty to draw attention specifically to this text because of its theological importance in Wesley's doctrine of the sacrament.

portrait of the dominion of God through the imagery related to this banquet:

Come, sinners, to the gospel-feast,
Let every soul be Jesu's guest,
Ye need not one be left behind,
For God hath bid all humankind.

Sent by my Lord, on you I call,
The invitation is to all.
Come all the world: come, sinner, thou,
All things in Christ are ready now.

Excused from coming to a feast!
Excused from being Jesu's guest!
From knowing *now* your sins forgiven,
From tasting *here* the joys of heaven!

Excused, alas! Why should ye be
From health, and life, and liberty,
From entering into glorious rest,
From leaning on your Savior's breast.

Come then ye souls, by sin oppressed,
Ye restless wanderers after rest,
Ye poor, and maimed, and halt, and blind,
In Christ an hearty welcome find.

My message as from God receive
Ye all may come to Christ, and live:
O let his love your hearts constrain,
Nor suffer him to die in vain.

His love is mighty to compel,
His conquering love consent to feel,
Yield to his love's resistless power,

And fight against your God no more.

This is the time, no more delay,
This is the acceptable day,
Come in, this moment, at his call,
And live for him who died for all. (*Redemption Hymns*, 63–66)

Questions for Consideration

1. What do Charles and John Wesley mean by "constant communion"?

2. How was the Wesleyan revival also a revival in the practice of the Eucharist?

3. How did the Wesley brothers and the early Methodists understand the Eucharist or Holy Communion?

4. What does "sacramental remembrance" truly entail for Charles Wesley?

5. What does Wesley mean when speaking of the "real presence" of Christ in the Eucharist?

6. How does Wesley's emphasis on Holy Communion as a "pledge of heaven and hope" enrich our understanding of, and relationship to, the "communion of the saints"?

7. In what ways does Wesley's view of the Great Supper communicate the nature of God's love and the practice of living a cruciform life?

eight

Dominion: Situated in God's Shalom

CHARLES WESLEY WAS SUCH a student of the Bible he could hardly have missed the emphasis on the kingdom of God throughout the biblical narrative, but particularly in the ministry of Jesus. "The concept of the Kingdom of God involves, in a real sense," claimed John Bright, "the total message of the Bible."[1] While Wesley seldom used language often used today with regard to this critical theme of scripture, his hymns and sacred poems address all the issues surrounding God's rule and reign—God's dominion. It would be pedantic simply to gather all Charles's references to the term *kingdom*, but the statistics are somewhat overwhelming. Simply to illustrate, in his two published volumes of *Scripture Hymns* the term appears more than 150 times. Likewise, in his manuscript hymns on Matthew's Gospel—a biblical document in which the kingdom of God figures quite prominently—Wesley appropriates the term in more than one hundred instances. While the term itself is important, greater significance attaches to the major themes related to God's dominion in the biblical witness and the process by which God resituates the faithful in God's shalom.

1. Bright, *Kingdom of God*, 7.

Given Charles's emphasis on kingdom, it should be no surprise that the petition in the Lord's Prayer—"Your kingdom come. Your will be done, on earth as it is in heaven" (Matt 6:10)—figures prominently in his hymns and serves as the signature text for this biblical theme. He refers to this verse explicitly sixteen times in the *Collection*. Wesley discerns a dual focus related to God's dominion in this text—the importance of both God's kingdom and God's will. St. Luke's version of the Lord's Prayer inspired Wesley to compose what will function as our signature hymn for the biblical theme of dominion. This sacred poem is actually a composite hymn, combining two lyrical paraphrases of Luke 11:2:

> Father of me, and all mankind,
>   And all the hosts above,
> Let every understanding mind
>   Unite to praise thy love,
> To know thy nature and thy name,
>   One God in Persons Three,
> And glorify the great I AM
>   Through all eternity.
>
> Thy kingdom come, with power and grace,
>   To every heart of man,
> Thy peace and joy, and righteousness,
>   In all our bosoms reign!
> Thy righteousness our sin keep down,
>   Thy peace our passions bind,
> And let us in thy joy unknown,
>   The first dominion find.
>
> The righteousness that never ends,
>   But makes an end of sin,
> The joy that human thought transcends,
>   Into our souls bring in,
> The kingdom of established peace,
>   Which can no more remove,

The perfect power of godliness,
The omnipotence of love. (*Scripture Hymns*, 2:220)

Charles yearns for all people to rediscover this "first dominion," which God's creatures rejected and ignored. As in his doctrine of redemption, restoration plays a central role in his concept
of Christ's kingdom. People, in his view, do not build the kingdom; rather, God must restore the rule of Christ. Believers receive
the kingdom into their hearts and then partner with God in this
work in the world. Wesley's hymn reflects multiple facets of God's
dominion, but he alludes primarily here to Romans 14:17—the
kingdom of God is righteousness, and peace, and joy. In his poetic
corpus he defines God's dominion along the lines of this important
trilogy frequently. To gain a better understanding of his "lyrical
kingdom theology" we will explore his concepts of the kingdom
of heart, the character of the kingdom, the church as a missional
community, and the "already but not yet" character of God's rule.

The Kingdom of the Heart

As Jesus's own teaching makes clear, the kingdom of God resides
in the human heart. Wesley's poetic rendering of Matthew 6:10 expresses his longing for God's dominion in the hearts of all people:

When shall thy Spirit reign
In every heart of man?
Father, bring the kingdom near,
Honor thy triumphant Son,
God of heaven, on earth appear,
Fix with us thy glorious throne. (*Scripture Hymns*, 2:142)

"Fix in every heart of man," he prays, "thine everlasting throne"
(*Scripture Hymns*, 1:160). Charles makes his appeal to the broken,
to those whose hearts are still turned in on themselves. If any are
to participate in God's rule, they must first turn their hearts to
God. Before turning their attention outward, they must first attend
to their deepest interior need. "Sinners, turn, believe, and find,"

Charles pleads, "the kingdom in your hearts" (MS Matthew, 113).
In the same hymn we read,

> God comes down on earth to reign,
> With dazzling majesty confessed:
> Every happy, pardoned man
> Contains him in his breast.

Charles's discussion of the kingdom of the heart reflects the
same apophatic/kataphatic rhythm that characterizes his spirituality. He connects the interior life of the spirit intimately with the
believer's engagement in "kingdom ministry." Urgency characterizes the singers' plea:

> I will, through grace I will;
> I do return to thee:
> Take, empty it, O Lord, and fill
> My heart with purity:
> For power I feebly pray;
> Thy kingdom now restore,
> Today, while it is called today,
> And I shall sin no more. (*Scripture Hymns*, 2:11)

Those who turn over their hearts to God for God's use receive
God's power both to do so and to live as God's children. Charles
reflects on the meaning of St. Paul's statement that "the kingdom
of God is not in word, but in power" (1 Cor 4:20). Whenever God
imparts the Spirit, he argues, "The kingdom restored is power in
our hearts" (*Scripture Hymns*, 2:291). But unlike the power of the
world, this power is that of Christ's passion, "The strength of salvation, / the virtue of love." Charles perceives a peculiar trajectory
related to this rule of God. God's dominion begins in the human
heart most certainly, but it extends into the church and then ex-
pands yet further to the poor. "For Methodists this internal transformation was not enough," observes Andrew Winckles. "The true
evidence of the kingdom of God in heart and life was in how it
worked outward into community."[2]

2. Winckles, "Kingdom of God."

Still the great God resides below,
(And all his faithful people know
  He will not from his church depart)
The Father, Son, and Spirit dwells,
His kingdom in the poor reveals,
  And fills with heaven the humble heart.
(*Scripture Hymns*, 1:167)

Christ inextricably binds righteousness, joy, and peace together with justice and compassion.

The Character of the Kingdom—Righteousness, Joy, and Peace

In his hymns related to the kingdom of God Wesley exploits all the stories and language provided by Jesus in his own teachings on this theme. Charles's manuscript hymns on the Gospels are replete with this dominion imagery. The kingdom is like leaven in a loaf of bread (Matt 13:33), exerting a catalytic influence in the heart:

That heavenly principle within,
  Doth it at once its power exert,
At once root out the seed of sin,
  And spread perfection through the heart?
No: but a gradual light it sends
  Diffusive thro' the faithful soul,
To actions, words, and thoughts extends,
  And slowly sanctifies the whole.
(MS Matthew, 163–64)

God will not let this "spark expire," Wesley maintains. God will ultimately "obtain the victory" and "fix the kingdom in my heart" (MS Matthew, 146). The kingdom is like a grain of mustard seed (Luke 13:19). Like the "minutest grain," it matures and will eventually "shoot up at once into a tree" (MS Luke, 201). The kingdom is like a treasure to be pursued above all else. Like Jesus, Charles admonishes the singer to place the highest priority on God's rule:

> I seek the kingdom first,
>   The gracious joy and peace,
> Thou knowest, I hunger, Lord, and thirst
>   After thy righteousness;
>   My chief, and sole desire
>   Thine image to regain,
> And then to join thy heavenly choir,
>   And with thine ancients reign. (*Scripture Hymns*, 2:145)

The kingdom comes to the meek. "O how unlike the kingdoms here / Thy kingdom opened in thine own!" According to Charles, the throne of Christ in the heart can only be supported by meekness, peace, lowly fear, and righteousness, and its fruit is "love invincibly Divine" (MS Matthew, 240–41). Wesley warns his followers, therefore, about the danger of riches in relation to the kingdom:

> Who wealth possesses here,
>   And is by wealth possessed,
> Can never in his sight appear
>   By whom the poor are blest. (MS Luke, 267)

This concern elicits one of Charles's most powerful lyrical statements related to the pursuit of God's kingdom:

> Not with outward pomp and state
>   Comes thy kingdom here below,
> Those that would be rich or great
>   Cannot its true nature know,
> The dim eyes of flesh and blood
>   Never can its glory see:
> But when I embrace my God,
>   Then I find thy throne in me.
>
> Love, the power of humble love
>   Constitutes thy kingdom here:

Never, never to remove
  Let it, Lord, in me appear,
Let the pure, internal grace
  Fill my new-created soul,
Peace, and joy, and righteousness,
    While eternal ages roll. (MS Luke, 251–52)

Note his reference here to the grand trilogy. In the kingdom of God peace displaces discord and anxiety, joy supplants sorrow and discouragement, and righteousness dislodges depravity and sin. While each of these constitutive elements of God's reign relate directly to the individual at a deeply personal level, they also have a critical social dimension. In a poetic reflection on Romans 14:17, Charles prays with the singer for the realization of these gifts:

Lord, I want thy power and peace,
  Power to make an end of sin,
Joy to bid my troubles cease,
  Righteousness to reign within:
Pure, and happy may I be;
  Then thy kingdom's come to me. (*Scripture Hymns*, 2:287)

The Character of the Kingdom—Justice and Compassion

Charles mandates that faithful disciples of Jesus translate the personal gifts of righteousness, joy, and peace into concrete acts of justice and compassion. In a hymn he composed for his wife on their wedding day (*HSP 1749*, 2:280–81), Charles affords a unique window into the aspects of Christian character shaped by the values of the kingdom.

Come, let us arise,
And press to the skies,
The summons obey,
My friend, my beloved, and hasten away!
The master of all

> For our service doth call,
>> And deigns to approve
> With smiles of acceptance our labor of love.

The hymn encourages bride and groom to be accountable to one another in love and good works as a performance of God's rule in their lives. Their common witness to the kingdom meant attending to those who were distressed, afflicted, and oppressed. Their kingdom work entailed relieving prisoners, receiving strangers, and supplying all their wants. Kingdom ministry included acts of justice and compassion.

Justice

Various forms of injustice clamored for attention in Wesley's day. His hymns encouraged commitment to God's vision of shalom and active engagement in ministries of justice. One of his *Hymns of Intercession for All Mankind*, in particular, paints a vivid portrait of a world gone wrong—but offers an alternative biblical vision for life as God intended it to be:

> Our earth we now lament to see
>> With floods of wickedness overflowed,
> With violence, wrong, and cruelty,
>> One wide-extended field of blood,
> Where men, like fiends, each other tear
> In all the hellish rage of war. (4)

The singer intercedes on behalf of humanity with regard to the atrocities associated with a fallen world. Charles calls upon Jesus to intervene:

> O might the universal Friend
>> This havoc of his creatures see!
> Bid our unnatural discord end,
>> Declare us reconciled in thee!
> Write kindness on our inward parts
> And chase the murderer from our hearts. (4)

He locates the hope for peace in the transformation of the human heart and calls on all faithful disciples of Jesus "to follow after peace, and prize / The blessings of thy righteous reign." This, and only this, will restore "the paradise of perfect love."

Isaiah's prophetic vision provides the imagery for many of his hymns that seek to promote this vision of shalom. His brilliant lyrical paraphrase of Isaiah 11:6–7 must suffice to illustrate the theme:

> Prince of universal peace,
>   Destroy the enmity,
> Bid our jars and discords cease,
>   Unite us all in thee.
> Cruel as wild beasts we are,
> Till vanquished by thy mercy's power,
> All, like wolves, each other tear,
>   And their own flesh devour.
>
> But if thou pronounce the word
>   That forms our souls again,
> Love and harmony restored
>   Throughout the earth shall reign;
> When thy wondrous love they feel,
> The human savages are tame,
>   Ravenous wolves, and leopards dwell
>   And stable with the lamb. (*Scripture Hymns*, 1:316)

Compassion

There is an amazing body of hymnody related to the poor in Wesley's collected works. "Perhaps the uniqueness of his contribution lies," Kimbrough argues, "in the way he opened for the church to remember its responsibility to the dispossessed of the earth."[3] Wesley "creates a hymnic, poetically remembered theology," he

3. Kimbrough, "Wesley and the Poor," 148.

claims, "that articulates the imperatives of ministry to the poor."[4] Charles's doctrine of the kingdom demonstrates God's love for the poor, their important role in the community of faith, and the responsibility of all faithful disciples to engage in advocacy for all who are dispossessed. The following hymn well illustrates both Charles's attitude toward the poor and the actions that faithful Christians should take on their behalf, all modeled after Jesus:

> The poor as Jesus' bosom friends,
>   The poor he makes his latest care,
> To all his followers commends,
>   And wills us on our hands to bear;
> The poor our dearest care we make,
>   And love them for our Savior's sake. (MS Acts, 421)

Charles often depicts the kingdom character of those whose lives have been conformed to the image of the compassionate Christ through their ministry alongside the marginalized. Mary Naylor was one such woman, an active leader of the Methodist society in Bristol noted for God's rule in her life:

> The golden rule she still pursued,
> And did to others as she would
>   Others should do to her;
> Justice composed her upright soul,
> Justice did all her thoughts control,
>   And formed her character.
>
> Affliction, poverty, disease,
> Drew out her soul in soft distress,
>   The wretched to relieve;
> In all the works of love employed,
> Her sympathizing soul enjoyed
>   The blessedness to give.

4. Ibid., 155.

A nursing mother to the poor,
For them she husbanded her store,
  Her life, her all, bestowed;
For them she labored day and night,
In doing good her whole delight,
  In copying after God. (*Funeral Hymns 1759*, 51, 53)

An affective experience of God's rule and an outward performance of the kingdom defined Wesley's doctrine of God's dominion. As Winckles has observed, the genius of Methodism in this regard was "a subjectivity founded not upon individual autonomy and rights but on the freedom to do God's will, to enact the kingdom on earth."[5]

The Role of the Church—Missional Community

From Wesley's perspective the church plays a major role in regard to God's dominion. He and his brother rediscovered a "mission-church paradigm" in their own day.[6] They believed that God designed the church as a redemptive community, a family that lives in and for God's vision of shalom in the world. God calls the church to bear witness to this dominion in every aspect of life. The church in this biblical paradigm draws committed Christian disciples perennially to Jesus and to one another in community for the purpose of spinning them out into the world in mission and service. The Wesleys built this vision of the church on the solid theological foundation we have already explored in previous chapters. Their missional practice mirrored their understanding of God—the loving Creator of all, active and at work in the world to save and restore all creation. They developed a holistic vision of mission and evangelism that refused to separate faith and works, personal salvation and social justice, physical and spiritual needs. Charles promoted this understanding of church through his hymns.

5. Winckles, "Kingdom of God."
6. See Chilcote, "Mission-Church Paradigm," 151–64.

> A charge to keep I have,
> A God to glorify,
> A never-dying soul to save,
> And fit it for the sky.
> To serve the present age,
> My calling to fulfill;
> O may it all my powers engage
> To do my Master's will! (*Scripture Hymns*, 1:58)

In an exceptional study of Charles Wesley's missiology, Tore Meistad demonstrated how "the transformation of the person becomes a part of the transformation of the entire cosmos."[7] As a consequence of Wesley's rediscovery, the early Methodists modeled their lives and their vision of the church after this pattern. Put quite simply, Charles believed that the church exists to perform or realize God's vision of the peaceable kingdom:

> Jesu, Lord, we look to thee,
> Let us in thy name agree;
> Show thyself the Prince of peace,
> Bid our jars forever cease.
>
> By thy reconciling love
> Every stumbling block remove,
> Each to each unite, endear:
> Come, and spread thy banner here!
>
> Let us each for other care,
> Each the other's burden bear;
> To thy church the pattern give,
> Show how true believers live. (*HSP* 1749, 1:248)

In the context of the church, faithful followers of Jesus experience the marks of the kingdom and participate in actions that shape kingdom character in their lives.

---

7. Meistad, "Missiology of Charles Wesley," 49.

One of Charles's eucharistic hymns elicits a profoundly missiological vision of this all-encompassing engagement of the disciple in God's reign (*HLS*, 129–30).

> If so low a child as I
>   May to thy great glory live,
> All my actions sanctify,
>   All my words and thoughts receive;
> Claim me for thy service, claim
> All I have and all I am.

The follower of Jesus asks God to claim every aspect of his or her life in a sacrifice that can only be described as covenantal. One can hear echoes of the baptismal covenant, perhaps, in Charles's use of language. Baptism signals the beginning of discipleship, that event in which God inaugurates each person into the kingdom of Christ. It also signals the commitment of the individual and the community to God's mission.

> Take my soul and body's powers,
>   Take my memory, mind, and will,
> All my goods, and all my hours,
>   All I know, and all I feel,
> All I think, and speak, and do;
> Take my heart—and make it new.

In hymns like this one Wesley cultivates a profound vision of servant vocation elicited by and shaped within the community of faith—the church—a missional conception of Christian discipleship summarized tersely in the phrase "Claim me for thy service."

God's Domain—"Already but Not Yet"

The church, like the individual disciple, strives for perfection. Perfection, however, is often elusive. The kingdom has come in Jesus Christ and yet the church still prays for it to come. With regard to the domain of God there is an "already but not yet" dynamic at work. George Eldon Ladd popularized this language in the 1950s, describing both a present and future dimension of the kingdom of God in scripture.[8] Charles drew the same conclusions, basically conceiving of a realm in which God rules in the present and a future fulfillment of God's dominion that is not yet fully realized. He describes both realities in his hymns.

He bears witness to the present rule of God in a lyrical reflection on Daniel 7:18 (*Scripture Hymns*, 2:63–64). The present kingdom, he argues, is already given to all the saints below. "It is not of this world, we know, / But comes with Christ from heaven." He celebrates the fact that God's people live in God's reign "before we reach the sky," and in the present moment "with Christ triumphant live." The church celebrates this present kingdom, partners with God to cultivate its values, and proclaims God's vision of shalom. Times of trouble, in particular, elicit Charles's hopes for the future, coming kingdom.

> We know that his word
> > And promise are past;
> Thy kingdom, O Lord,
> > Shall triumph at last:
> The kingdoms before thee
> > And nations shall fall,
> And all men adore thee,
> > The monarch of all. (*HTT 1744*, 9)

Daniel's description of the God of heaven who destroys, breaks in pieces, and consumes all other kingdoms provides the graphic language that suits Charles's vision well. "Let thy kingdom come," he prays. "All these worldly powers o'erthrow, / And scatter, and consume!" And he anticipates a divine monarchy that will be "founded in perpetual grace" (*Scripture Hymns*, 2:58–59).

> Father, by right divine,
> > Assert the kingdom thine;
> Jesus, power of God, subdue

8. See Ladd, *The Gospel of the Kingdom.*

Thine own universe to thee;
  Spirit of grace and glory too,
    Reign through all eternity. (*Scripture Hymns*, 2:143)

Sometimes the present and future coalesce in Wesley's poetry. The imagery of the heavenly banquet in his eucharistic hymns, in particular, evokes this eschatological fusion.

At the table the community of faith dwells, as it were, in both kingdoms, present and future. Only a thin veil separates the one from the other.

The church triumphant in thy love
  Their mighty joys we know,
They sing the Lamb in hymns above,
  And we in hymns below.

Thee in thy glorious realm they praise,
  And bow before thy throne,
We in the kingdom of thy grace,
  The kingdoms are but one. (*HLS*, 84)

Gathered around the table for "thy great kingdom feast," the faithful feel God's promise of "eternal rest." "Yet still an higher seat," Wesley proclaims, "we in thy kingdom claim."

That glorious heavenly prize
  We surely shall attain,
And in the palace of the skies
  With thee forever reign. (*HLS*, 84)

Permanency characterizes God's dominion—God's rule and reign of perfect love.

Earthly kingdoms soon decline,
  Totter, fall, and pass away;
Permanent, O Christ, is thine,
  Cannot molder, or decay;
Every other power o'rethrown

Shall its destined period prove,
Thy dominion stands alone,
Fixed as thine eternal love. (MS Luke, 7)

Questions for Consideration

1. In what ways does Charles Wesley's lyrical theology speak to the rule of God in the life of the believer and the world? What are the key concepts Wesley uses to communicate God's dominion?

2. How does Charles Wesley's discussion of the kingdom of the heart reflect the same "apophatic/kataphatic" rhythm of his spirituality?

3. How does Wesley understand the nature of God's power in relation to Christ's passion on the cross and to the practice of ministry among the poor?

4. What is the relationship between the character of God's kingdom and the virtues of the Christian life?

5. How did the early Methodists connect compassion and justice in service with and to the poor?

6. How are the inward rule of God's grace and the outward performance of God's kingdom related with respect to mission in the world?

7. What is the mission of the church in relation to God's kingdom?

8. In what way does baptism signal the inauguration of Christ's rule in the life of the believer and the movement toward mission among the faithful?

9. What does it mean to say that God's kingdom is "already, but not yet"? How is this tension to inform the practice of ministry, especially when celebrating the Eucharist?

nine

Perfection: Abiding in God's Love

EVERY TIME CHARLES WESLEY celebrated the sacrament of Holy Communion or participated in the Anglican eucharistic liturgy, through the Collect for Purity he prayed with the community to perfectly love God. The quest for perfect love, or Christian perfection, defined his life and shaped his poetry more than any other single element. Wesley's religious verse reflects a bi-focal understanding of perfection rooted in the two great commandments of Jesus, what could be called the twin dimensions of sanctification: holiness of heart, or love of God, and holiness of life, or love of neighbor (Matt 22:37–39). Faith, he was convinced, leads to love in the Christian life if it is authentic, and to be loving or holy is to be truly happy. The final biblical theme in his lyrical theology that we will explore reflects his belief that all Christians can grow into the perfect love God has promised in Christ.

Christian perfection was, and still is, one of the most distinctive but misunderstood Wesleyan doctrines. With the therapeutic focus in Wesley's way of salvation, it was natural for him to ask two critical questions: (1) How fully can love be realized and how fully can sin be purged in this life? (2) Does this experience come in crisis or by means of a process of maturation in love? His distinctive answer was that there is a possibility of entire sanctification, or Christian perfection, in this life. To put it quite simply, he trusted that faithful Christians could attain the goal of life in life, even if at the point of death, and this was his settled viewpoint. The realization of perfect love, he also believed, entails a lengthy process of growth and never-ending reliance on Christ. Perfection, holiness of heart and life, entire sanctification, full salvation, perfect love are simply so many terms to denote one thing—loving God above all else, and all else in God.

Charles developed his vision of Christian perfection, as did his brother, on the basis of his study of scripture. But his mature view of perfect love resonates soundly with the vision of the early church fathers. His preferred poetic language was that of "perfect love." His concept of love was extremely dynamic, not so much a state attained, nor something absolute, but something always improvable. The main and enduring stress of his doctrine of perfection, and something upon which he and his brother agreed, was the potential triumph of God's grace and the power of a whole-hearted love of God and neighbor to displace all lesser loves and to overcome the remains of sin. He describes perfection as conformity to Christ:

> Lord, we believe, and wait the hour
>   Which all thy great salvation brings:
> The Spirit of love, and health, and power
>   Shall come, and make us priests and kings;
> Thou wilt perform thy faithful word,
> The servant shall be as his Lord.
>
> The promise stands forever sure,
>   And we shall in thine image shine,
> Partakers of a nature pure,
>   Holy, and perfect, and divine,
> In Spirit joined to thee the Son,
> As thou art with thy Father one. (HSP 1742, 234)

123

The quest for love, purity, righteousness, and union with God characterize Wesley's view of this high calling in Christ Jesus. The constitutive elements of the *theosis*—likeness to or union with God—that he taught include restoration, Christlikeness, and radiance.

The Quest for Love

It is not too much to say that, once Wesley had experienced the unconditional love of God in Christ and developed a clear vision of his purpose in life as a child of God, he made the pursuit of this holiness his primary goal. "His subsequent spiritual life," as J. Ernest Rattenbury stated so succinctly, "might be summed up compendiously in one phrase: 'a quest for love.'"[1] Perhaps no verses he penned ever expressed his passion about this quest more than the concluding stanzas of a hymn written soon after his poignant experience of God's love in May 1738:

> To love is all my wish,
> I only live for this:
> Grant me, Lord, my heart's desire,
> There by faith forever dwell:
> This I always will require
> Thee and only thee to feel.

> Thy power I pant to prove
> Rooted and fixed in love,
> Strengthened by thy Spirit's might,
> Wise to fathom things divine,
> What the length and breadth and height,
> What the depth of love like thine.

> Ah! Give me this to know
> With all thy saints below.

1. Rattenbury, *Evangelical Doctrines*, 278.

Swells my soul to compass thee,
Gasps in thee to live and move,
Filled with all the deity,
All immersed and lost in love! (*HSP 1739*, 169)

Wesley's signature text for the theme of perfection is 1 John 4:18, "There is no fear in love, but perfect love casts out fear; for fear has to do with punishment, and whoever fears has not reached perfection in love." His poetic paraphrase of this passage reveals the nature of the love that was central to his quest:

There is no fear in love,
No base tormenting fear,
But that which thrills the host above,
When Jesu's wounds appear!
The highest joy transcends
To saints triumphant given,
The seraph's loftiest songs suspends,
And makes a silent heaven! (*Scripture Hymns*, 2:402)

He came to believe that no force in the universe is more powerful than love. Love is more powerful than hate. Love triumphs over evil. Love can conquer the disobedient heart. Love never coerces. Love never fails. Charles prayed consistently for God's love to fill his soul—and not his soul only, but the soul of every child of God.

His hymn "Against Hope, Believing in Hope" celebrates the experience of divine love and the purifying work of the Holy Spirit—the way in which the children of God both know and feel God's love in their lives.

Jesus, thine all-victorious love
Shed in my heart abroad;
Then shall my feet no longer rove,
Rooted and fixed in God.

O! that in me the sacred fire
Might now begin to glow;

> Burn up the dross of base desire
> And make the mountains flow!
>
> Refining fire, go through my heart,
> Illuminate my soul;
> Scatter thy life through every part
> And sanctify the whole.
>
> My steadfast soul, from falling free,
> Can now no longer move;
> Jesus is all the world to me,
> And all my heart is love. (*HSP 1740*, 157–58)

The love of God in the soul is like a fire that converts, softens, melts, pierces, breaks, glows, burns, consumes, refines, illuminates, fills, and sanctifies the whole person. Wesley's prayer is that all might experience this in life—that their quest might carry them home.

Purity: Holiness of Heart

Charles most likely drew his inspiration for a hymn still sung by many today from the famous collect of the Anglican *Book of Common Prayer* quoted above and its scriptural point of reference (Ps 51:10). This signature hymn for perfection provides one of the most mature expressions of his vision of a life perfected in holiness and love:

> O for a heart to praise my God,
> A heart from sin set free!
> A heart that always feels thy blood,
> So freely spilt for me!
>
> A heart in every thought renewed
> And full of love divine,
> Perfect, and right, and pure, and good,
> A copy, Lord, of thine.

Thy nature, dearest Lord, impart;
  Come quickly from above;
  Write thy new name upon my heart,
    Thy new, best name of Love. (*HSP 1742*, 30–31)

In this hymn Wesley maintains the intimate connection between holiness and the human heart. He assumes that whatever is
written on the heart reflects the true character of the person. His
hymn celebrates the heart of the believer—the heart upon which
God has written the law of love. God writes on the heart, shapes
the character, forms the disciple, restores the image of Christ in
the child. While his poetic exposition of Psalm 51 addresses the
aspiration of perfect love in the believer, Wesley focuses the singer
on the idea of God's steadfast love. As in all aspects of his theology,
God remains prevenient. As S T Kimbrough has observed with
regard to this hymn, "It is through the *steadfast love of God* that we
are granted pure hearts. It is *God's love* that enables and sustains
purity of heart. There is no way to purity and holiness without
love!"[2]

Charles never wavered from this conviction and celebrated
the liberation secured through the purifying process of sanctification. Neither did he ever lose hope of feeling the efficacy of God's
action on his behalf, both in justification and in sanctification. He
longs to experience holiness not only as an intellectual affirmation but as emotional vitality, to both know and feel the power
of God's transforming love in the depth of his being. The concept
of renewal occupies a central place in Wesley's articulation of the
ideal. Through the refining process of sanctification God renews
the image of Christ in the believer. God transcribes or copies the
mind, perfection, righteousness, purity, and goodness of Jesus
into the life of the apprentice. God imbues those open to the Holy
Spirit with Christ's—with God's—own nature: "thy new, best name
of Love."

---

2. Kimbrough, *Heart to Praise My God*, 140.

The theme of purity of heart pervades a special manuscript collection of thirty-four Wesley "Hymns for Love." The first stanza of the opening hymn sets the tone:

> O for a spark of heavenly fire
> From the Redeemer's throne
> The pure, and permanent desire
> Of loving Him alone! (MS Hymns for Love, 41)

"Peace and purity impart," Charles prays. "Speak thy name into my heart" (58). He equates the images of purity with light, drawing a sharp contrast between the darkness of the unredeemed soul and the glory of the sanctified child of God.

> Brightness of the Deity,
> Christ, into my darkness shine,
> That I may the glory see,
> Thee the Light and life divine
> Thee throughout my darkness prove
> Pure, unutterable Love. (58)

In all these hymns he appeals to God for both purity of heart and righteousness of life.

> Purest love, and joy, and peace
> Everlasting righteousness,
> All the good with Christ bestowed
> All the plenitude of God,
> Bring into my newborn soul,
> Consecrate, and fill the whole. (54–55)

Righteousness—Holiness of Life

To be truly filled with perfect love means that those qualities which flow from Christ's holiness and righteousness flow through the sanctified believer in loving attitudes and actions towards others. Unless the love of God elicits the fullest possible love of neighbor, that love remains disingenuous. Abundant life consists in aversion to sin of every kind and an inclination to do good at every opportunity:

> I only live to win
> Thy pure and heavenly mind,
> Like Thee averse from every sin,
> To every good inclined:
> O that I now with Thee
> Thy nature might possess,
> Thy hatred of iniquity,
> Thy love of righteousness! (MS Hymns for Love, 44–45)

The hatred of everything antithetical to God and the love of everything good and right and true characterize the Christian perfected in love. To be perfected in love meant to be employed in Jesus's cause—loving others the way he loves all.

A proper love of neighbor—holiness of life—begs for illustration from real life, and Charles often provided poignant portraits of those he believed had been perfected in love. The classic example of this comes from an incident in May 1741. He visited Mrs. Hooper at her deathbed and was so moved by her purity and righteousness that he exclaimed, "This is that holiness, or absolute resignation, or Christian perfection!"[3] He immediately drafted a lyrical eulogy in her remembrance:

> In her no spot of sin remained,
> To shake her confidence in God,
> The victory here she more than gained,
> Triumphant through her Savior's blood.
>
> She died in sure and steadfast hope,
> By Jesus wholly sanctified,
> Her perfect spirit she gave up,
> And sunk into his arms, and died. (HSP 1742, 125)

---

3. Kimbrough and Newport, *Manuscript Journal*, 1:304 (May 6, 1741).

Theosis—Participation in the Divine Nature

The phrase "restoration of the image of Christ" reflects the heart of Wesley's vision of perfection. Like other aspects of his soteriology, in addition to the preeminent witness of scripture, he owed a debt to many spiritual forebears for this concept. His view of perfect love, as noted earlier, bears a striking resemblance to the vision rooted in Patristic sources. As Kimbrough has acknowledged, "While one might labor to find numerous quotations of the Early Fathers in Charles Wesley's poetry, his theology exudes the spirit of much of their theology."[4] Peter Bouteneff finds resonance between Gregory of Nyssa and Charles Wesley, in particular, around the "themes of salvation as restoration, and as change and movement from glory to glory."[5] The concluding stanza of Wesley's famous *Redemption Hymn*, "Love Divine, All Loves Excelling"—some of the most beloved lines in all his poetic production—celebrates this lofty goal:

> Finish then thy new creation,
>> Pure and sinless let us be,
> Let us see thy great salvation,
>> Perfectly restored in thee;
> Changed from glory into glory,
>> Till in heaven we take our place,
> Till we cast our crowns before thee,
>> Lost in wonder, love, and praise! (12)

Kimbrough notes how the concern of *theosis*—participation in the divine nature—"surfaces time and again in Charles Wesley's poetry in concert with many of the Early Fathers of the Church."[6] He illustrates this connection with an example from Wesley's *Nativity Hymns* in which the twin themes of incarnation and restoration find profound expression:

4. Kimbrough, *Lyrical Theology*, 88.
5. Bouteneff, "All Creation in United Thanksgiving," 194.
6. Kimbrough, *Lyrical Theology*, 89.

Made flesh for our sake,
That we might partake
The nature divine,
    And again in his image, his holiness shine;

And while we are here,
Our King shall appear,
His Spirit impart,
    And form his full image of love in our heart. (12)

It is dangerous to minimize the complexity of this concept of *theosis*, but three themes, in particular, find repeated expression in Wesley's verse: the claim that the Spirit restores the image of Christ in the believer, that transformed disciples of Jesus will be like him, and that this kind of transformation enables them to shine to the glory of God.

Restoration

The Spirit restores the image of Christ in the believer. Perfection means restoration.

Father, Son, and Holy-Ghost,
    In council join again
To restore thine image, lost
    By frail apostate man:
O might I thy form express,
    Through faith begotten from above,
Stamped with real holiness,
    And filled with perfect love! (*Scripture Hymns*, 1:4)

While believers engage in a quest for holiness, Charles couches the restoration of the image of Christ in passive language: "Let us, to perfect love restored, / Thy image here retrieve" (*Scripture Hymns*, 2:89). The child of God does not manufacture but receives the image.

Wesley also employs a unique expression to define the outcome of God's restorative process. He describes the fully restored disciple as a transcript of the Trinity. This is one of his most potent metaphors related to *theosis*. In a lyrical eulogy Charles prepared on the occasion of Mrs. Lefevre's death, he affords this inspirational portrait:

> She *was* (what words can never paint)
> A spotless soul, a sinless saint,
>> In perfect love renewed,
> A mirror of the deity,
> A transcript of the One in Three,
>> A temple filled with God. (*Funeral Hymns 1759*, 47)

In one of his *Trinity Hymns* Charles explains the way in which this therapeutic transcription serves to honor and bring praise to the Three-One God:

> Remember thy Creators, God
>> In Persons Three confessed,
> Who raised thee up a breathing clod,
>> And with his name impressed:
> The Persons Three in council joined
>> To make his earth-born son;
> And, stamped with his immortal mind,
>> He claims thee for his own.
>
> He challenges thy youthful days
>> Who did thy being give:
> Created for his only praise,
>> For him rejoice to live;
> Transcript of holiness divine,
>> The Triune God proclaim,
> And spirit, and soul, and flesh resign
>> To glorify his name. (63)

While the way in which the faithful are transformed into the divine nature remains a mystery, nevertheless, Charles writes with fervent zeal about the transparent character of the transformed child of God.

Christlikeness

Transformed disciples of Jesus will be like him.[7] Perfection means Christlikeness. Those who bear the image of Christ conform to him in mind and life. In a journal entry dated November 4, 1737, Wesley records that he "heard an excellent sermon at St. Antholin's on holiness, or likeness to God."[8] He enunciates this central theme in a unique formulation of Matthew 10:25, "It is enough for the disciple to be like the teacher":

> My spirit meek, my will resigned,
> Lowly as thine shall be my mind,
> *The servant shall be as his Lord.*
> (*HSP 1742*, 170; italics added)

In another hymn he explicitly connects this restoration with conformity to Christ:

> We rest on His word
> We shall here be restored
> To His image; *the servant shall be as his Lord.*
> (*HSP 1749*, 2:179; italics added)

For Charles, this call to conformity to Christ defines the disciple— it characterizes the Christian who is altogether God's—and it also reflects God's promise. In virtually every hymn in which this phrase appears, it implies both a demand and a gift. "I stay me on thy faithful word," cries the follower of Christ groaning for full redemption. "The servant shall be as his Lord" (*HSP 1742*, 80). In the hymn "Prisoners of hope" this statement of vocation and promise functions as the refrain for the concluding stanzas:

---

7. In this section I develop themes first explored in an article titled "'Claim Me for Thy Service,'" 69–85.

8. Kimbrough and Newport, *Manuscript Journal*, 1:93.

Thou wilt perform thy faithful word:
"The servant shall be as his Lord."

We only hang upon thy word,
"The servant shall be as his Lord." (*HSP 1742*, 234)

But what does it mean to be like Jesus, according to Wesley?

The central place that Wesley gives to the kenotic hymn of Philippians provides a clue. So we come full circle here to where we began with the incarnation in chapter 1. In Charles's poetic exposition of Philippians 2:5, in successive stanzas of a hymn, he describes this mind in vivid detail as quiet, heavenly, humble, gentle, patient, noble, spotless, loving, thankful, and constant, and he concludes the hymn in confident affirmation of God's promise:

I shall fully be restored
To the image of my Lord,
Witnessing to all mankind,
Jesu's is a PERFECT mind. (*HSP 1742*, 223)

He takes this image a step further in a composite hymn in which he conjoins the "mind" of Philippians 2 with the "action" of James 1:

Thy mind throughout my life be shown,
  While listening to the wretch's cry,
The widow's and the orphan's groan,
  On mercy's wings I swiftly fly
The poor and helpless to relieve,
My life, my all, for them to give. (*Scripture Hymns*, 2:380)

Perhaps no hymn better expresses the character of the disciple whose mind is conformed to that of Christ than Charles's lyrical paraphrase of the Beatitudes:

Come, thou holy God and true!
Come, and my whole heart renew;
Take me now, possess me whole,
Form the Savior in my soul.

Happy soul, whose active love
Emulates the blessed above,
In thy every action seen,
Sparkling from the soul within.

Raiment thou to all that need,
To the hungry dealest thy bread,
To the sick thou givest relief,
Soothest the hapless prisoner's grief.

Love, which willeth all should live,
Love, which all to all would give,
Love, that over all prevails,
Love, that never, never fails. (*HSP 1749*, 1:38–39)

Radiance

Those who are fully conformed to the image of Christ shine to God's glory. Perfection means radiance.

God of all sufficient grace,
My God in Christ thou art;
Bid me walk before thy face,
Till I am pure in heart,
Till transformed through faith divine
I gain that perfect love unknown,
Bright in all thine image shine,
By putting on thy Son. (*Scripture Hymns*, 1:19)

The shining lives of God's restored children have a critical evangelistic role in the unfolding of God's reign. Light attracts; those who radiate the love of God draw others into the reign of God, as Wesley proclaims in this "Morning Hymn":

Clothed with Christ aspire to shine,
Radiance he of light divine;
Beam of the eternal beam,

He in God, and God in him!
Strive we him in us to see,
Transcript of the deity. (*HSP 1739*, 178)

For Wesley, Christ is the true and only light of the world whose radiance transcends all darkness, and when it floods the soul, all manner of darkness vanishes. He prays for the in-breaking of the glorious light of the One "whose glory fills the skies":

Visit then this soul of mine,
   Pierce the gloom of sin, and grief,
Fill me, radiancy divine,
   Scatter all my unbelief,
More and more thyself display
Shining to the perfect day. (*HSP 1740*, 25)

The biblical themes of Charles Wesley's lyrical theology—the doctrines of incarnation, redemption, repentance, justification, sanctification, prayer, communion, dominion, and perfection—all point to a God of pure, unbounded love—to a love that exceeds all loves. Wesley celebrates this bedrock of his life and the foundation of his lyrical theology in the incomparable hymn "Wrestling Jacob":

Pure UNIVERSAL LOVE thou art,
To me, to all thy mercies move,
Thy nature, and thy name is love (*HSP 1742*, 117).

Questions for Consideration

1. What does the author mean when he writes that Charles Wesley's religious verse reflects a "bi-focal" understanding of Christian perfection? How is this "bi-focal" understanding demonstrated in his lyrical theology?

2. What is Christian perfection, and how does Charles Wesley employ this concept throughout his writings?

3. How does Charles Wesley describe perfection? What key characteristics or virtues speak to the life of perfection or entire sanctification?

4. What is the relationship between perfecting grace and the holiness of heart and life? How do Wesley's hymns communicate the role of the Holy Spirit imparting the benefits of Christ's love to the believer?

5. What are some of the examples of "perfect love" Wesley uses to illustrate the life of holiness and righteousness?

6. What is *theosis*? How do Charles and John Wesley utilize this theological concept from the Patristic sources to describe the ways followers of Christ participate in the divine nature? How is such a concept related to the goal of perfection in the Christian life?

7. What three theological themes of Wesley are often repeated and intentionally related when speaking of *theosis*?

8. What does the term *transcript* of the Trinity entail? How is the life of a believer to be a transcript of holiness divine? Is such a term helpful? If so, why?

9. How do the hymns and poetry of Charles Wesley express the pure, unbounded love of God?

Bibliography

Anselm. *Cur Deus Homo*. In *A Scholastic Miscellany: Anselm to Ockham*, edited and translated by Eugene R. Fairweather, 100–183. Philadelphia: Westminster, 1956.

Baillie, D. M. *God Was in Christ*. New York: Scribner's, 1948.

Beck, Brian E. "Rattenbury Revisited: The Theology of Charles Wesley's Hymns." *Epworth Review* 26 (1999) 71–81.

Begbie, Jeremy S. *Resounding Truth: Christian Wisdom in the World of Music*. Grand Rapids: Baker Academic, 2007.

Berger, Teresa. *Theology in Hymns? A Study of the Relationship of Doxology and Theology according to* A Collection of Hymns for the People Called Methodists *(1780)*. Translated by Timothy E. Kimbrough. Nashville: Kingswood, 1995.

Borgen, Ole E. *John Wesley on the Sacraments: A Theological Study*. Grand Rapids: Zondervan, 1986.

Bouteneff, Peter. "All Creation in United Thanksgiving: Gregory of Nyssa and the Wesleys on Salvation." In *Orthodox and Wesleyan Spirituality*, edited by S T Kimbrough Jr., 189–201. Crestwood, NY: St. Vladimir's Seminary Press, 2002.

Bowmer, John C. *The Sacrament of the Lord's Supper in Early Methodism*. London: Dacre, 1951.

Bright, John. *The Kingdom of God: The Biblical Concept and Its Meaning for the Church*. New York: Abingdon-Cokesbury, 1953.

Campbell, Ted A. "Charles Wesley, *Theologos*." In *Charles Wesley: Life, Literature & Legacy*, edited by Kenneth G. C. Newport and Ted A. Campbell, 264–78. Peterborough: Epworth, 2007.

Chilcote, Paul W. "'All the Image of Thy Love': Charles Wesley's Vision of the One Thing Needful." *Proceedings of The Charles Wesley Society* 18 (2014) 21–40.

———. "Charles Wesley and Christian Practices." *Proceedings of The Charles Wesley Society* 12 (2008) 35–47.

————. "Charles Wesley and the Language of Faith." In *Charles Wesley: Life, Literature & Legacy*, edited by Kenneth G. C. Newport and Ted A. Campbell, 299–319. Peterborough: Epworth, 2007.

————. "Charles Wesley's Lyrical Credo." *Proceedings of The Charles Wesley Society* 15 (2011) 41–67.

————. "'Claim Me for Thy Service': Charles Wesley's Vision of Servant Vocation." *Proceedings of The Charles Wesley Society* 11 (2006–7) 69–85.

————. "A Faith That Sings: The Renewing Power of Lyrical Theology." In *The Wesleyan Tradition: A Paradigm for Renewal*, edited by Paul W. Chilcote, 148–62. Nashville: Abingdon, 2002.

————. "The Mission-Church Paradigm of the Wesleyan Revival." In *World Mission in the Wesleyan Spirit*, edited by Darrell L. Whiteman and Gerald H. Anderson, 151–64. Franklin, TN: Providence House, 2009.

Hildebrandt, Franz, and Oliver Beckerlegge, eds. *A Collection of Hymns for the Use of the People Called Methodists*. Works of John Wesley 7. Oxford: Clarendon, 1983.

Kimbrough, S T, Jr. "Charles Wesley and a Window to the East." In *Charles Wesley: Life, Literature & Legacy*, edited by Kenneth G. C. Newport and Ted A. Campbell, 165–83. Peterborough: Epworth, 2007.

————. "Charles Wesley and the Poor." In *The Portion of the Poor: Good News to the Poor in the Wesleyan Tradition*, edited by M. Douglas Meeks, 147–67. Nashville: Kingswood, 1995.

————. "Charles Wesley's Lyrical Commentary on the Holy Scriptures." In *Orthodox and Wesleyan Scriptural Understanding and Practice*, edited by S T Kimbrough Jr., 171–206. Crestwood, NY: St. Vladimir's Seminary Press, 2005.

————. "Charles Wesley's Understanding of the Nature of the Church." In *Orthodox and Wesleyan Ecclesiology*, edited by S T Kimbrough Jr., 129–47. Crestwood, NY: St. Vladimir's Seminary Press, 2007.

————. *A Heart to Praise My God: Wesley Hymns for Today*. Nashville: Abingdon, 1996.

————. "*Kenosis* in the Nativity Hymns of Ephrem the Syrian and Charles Wesley." In *Orthodox and Wesleyan Spirituality*, edited by S T Kimbrough Jr., 262–85. Crestwood, NY: St. Vladimir's Seminary Press, 2002.

————. *Lost in Wonder: Charles Wesley, the Meaning of His Hymns Today*. Nashville: Upper Room, 1987.

————. *The Lyrical Theology of Charles Wesley: A Reader*. Eugene, OR: Cascade, 2011.

Kimbrough, S T, Jr., and Kenneth G. C. Newport, eds. *The Manuscript Journal of the Reverend Charles Wesley, M.A.* 2 vols. Nashville: Kingswood, 2008.

Ladd, George Eldon. *The Gospel of the Kingdom: Scriptural Studies in the Kingdom of God*. Grand Rapids: Eerdmans, 1959.

Langford, Thomas A. "Charles Wesley as Theologian." In *Charles Wesley: Poet and Theologian*, edited by S T Kimbrough Jr., 97–105. Nashville: Kingswood, 1992.

Lawson, John. *The Wesley Hymns as a Guide to Scriptural Teaching.* Grand Rapids: Francis Asbury, 1987.

Meistad, Tore. "The Missiology of Charles Wesley: An Introduction." *Proceedings of The Charles Wesley Society* 5 (1998) 37–60.

Newport, Kenneth G. C., ed. *The Sermons of Charles Wesley: A Critical Edition.* New York: Oxford University Press, 2001.

Newton, John A. "Brothers in Arms: The Partnership of John and Charles Wesley." In *Charles Wesley: Life, Literature & Legacy,* edited by Kenneth G. C. Newport and Ted A. Campbell, 58–69. Peterborough: Epworth, 2007.

Outler, Albert C., ed. *John Wesley.* New York: Oxford University Press, 1964.

Rattenbury, J. Ernest. *The Eucharistic Hymns of John and Charles Wesley.* London: Epworth, 1948.

———. *The Evangelical Doctrines of Charles Wesley's Hymns.* London: Epworth, 1941.

Stevick, Daniel B. *The Altar's Fire: Charles Wesley's Hymns on the Lord's Supper, 1745.* Peterborough: Epworth, 2005.

Tabraham, Barrie W. *Brother Charles.* Peterborough: Epworth, 2003.

Telford, John, ed. *The Letters of the Rev. John Wesley, A.M.* 8 vols. London: Epworth, 1931.

Tyson, John R., ed. *Charles Wesley: A Reader.* New York: Oxford University Press, 1989.

———. *Charles Wesley on Sanctification: A Biographical and Theological Study.* Grand Rapids: Francis Asbury, 1986.

———. "'I Preached at the Cross, as usual': Charles Wesley and Redemption." In *Charles Wesley: Life, Literature & Legacy,* edited by Kenneth G. C. Newport and Ted A. Campbell, 204–28. Peterborough: Epworth, 2007.

———. "The Theology of Charles Wesley's Hymns." *Wesleyan Theological Journal* 44 (2007) 58–75.

Wainwright, Geoffrey. "Charles Wesley and Calvinism." In *Charles Wesley: Life, Literature & Legacy,* edited by Kenneth G. C. Newport and Ted A. Campbell, 184–203. Peterborough: Epworth, 2007.

Wesley, Charles. *Funeral Hymns.* N.p., n.p., [1746]; abbrev, *Funeral Hymns.*

———. *Funeral Hymns.* London: Strahan, 1759; abbrev, *Funeral Hymns 1759.*

———. *Hymns and Sacred Poems.* 2 vols. Bristol: Farley, 1749; abbrev, *HSP 1749.*

———. *Hymns for the Nativity of Our Lord.* London: Strahan, 1744; abbrev, *Nativity Hymns.*

———. *Hymns for the Use of Families.* Bristol: Pine, 1767; abbrev, *Family Hymns.*

———. *Hymns for Times of Trouble.* N.p., n.p., [1744]; abbrev, *HTT.*

———. *Hymns for Times of Trouble and Persecution.* London: Strahan, 1744; abbrev, *HTTP.*

———. *Hymns of Intercession for All Mankind.* Bristol: Farley, 1758; abbrev, *Intercession Hymns.*

———. *Hymns on God's Everlasting Love*. Bristol: Farley, 1741; abbrev, *Love Hymns 1741*.

———. *Hymns on God's Everlasting Love*. London: Strahan, 1742; abbrev, *Love Hymns 1742*.

———. *Hymns on the Trinity*. Bristol: Pine, 1767; abbrev, *Trinity Hymns*.

———. Manuscript Hymns for Love; abbrev, MS Hymns for Love.

———. Manuscript Hymns on the Acts of the Apostles; abbrev, MS Acts.

———. Manuscript Hymns on the Gospel of St. Luke; abbrev, MS Luke.

———. Manuscript Hymns on the Gospel of St. Matthew; abbrev, MS Matthew.

———. Manuscript Scriptural Hymns (Old Testament), 1783; abbrev, MS Hymns OT.

———. Manuscript Scriptural Hymns (New Testament), 1783; abbrev, MS Hymns NT.

———. "Promise of Sanctification." Edited by Randy Maddox. Duke Center for Studies in the Wesleyan Tradition. https://divinity.duke.edu/sites/divinity.duke.edu/files/documents/cswt/08_Promise_of_Sanctification_%281741%29_Mod.pdf.

———. "The Promise of Sanctification." In John Wesley, *Christian Perfection: A Sermon*, 44–48. London: Strahan, 1741; abbrev, Sanctification.

———. *Short Hymns on Select Passages of the Holy Scriptures*. 2 vols. Bristol: Farley, 1762; abbrev, *Scripture Hymns*.

Wesley, Charles [and John?]. *Hymns for those that seek, and those that have Redemption in the Blood of Jesus Christ*. London: Strahan, 1747; abbrev, *Redemption Hymns*.

Wesley, John, and Charles Wesley. *A Collection of Hymns, for the Use of the People Called Methodists*. London: Paramore, 1780; abbrev, *Collection*.

———. *Hymns and Sacred Poems*. London: Strahan, 1739; abbrev, *HSP 1739*.

———. *Hymns and Sacred Poems*. London: Strahan, 1740; abbrev, *HSP 1740*.

———. *Hymns and Sacred Poems*. Bristol: Farley, 1742; abbrev, *HSP 1742*.

———. *Hymns of Petition and Thanksgiving for the Promise of the Father*. Bristol: Farley, 1746; abbrev, *HPT*.

———. *Hymns on the Lord's Supper*. Bristol: Farley, 1745; abbrev, *HLS*.

Winckles, Andrew. "Kingdom of God—Kingdom of Man: Freedom, Identity, and Justice in Charles Wesley and William Blake." Unpublished paper presented at the North American Society for the Study of Romanticism Conference, Park City, Utah, August 12, 2011.

Yrigoyen, Charles. *Praising the God of Grace: The Theology of Charles Wesley's Hymns*. Nashville: Abingdon, 2005.

68287474R00100

Made in the USA
San Bernardino, CA
01 February 2018